THE BANSHEE

THE BANSHEE

ELLIOT O'DONNELL

ISBN: 978-93-90198-66-5

Published: -

LECTOR HOUSE LLP

LECTOR HOUSE LLP
E-MAIL: lectorpublishing@gmail.com

THE BANSHEE

BY

ELLIOT O'DONNELL

AUTHOR OF
"HAUNTED PLACES IN ENGLAND," "THE IRISH ABROAD,"
"TWENTY YEARS EXPERIENCES AS A GHOST HUNTER,"
ETC., ETC.

CONTENTS

Chapter   *Page*

   I. THE DEFINITION AND ORIGIN OF BANSHEES 1

   II. SOME HISTORICAL BANSHEES .5

   III. THE MALEVOLENT BANSHEE 11

   IV. THE BANSHEE ABROAD 18

   V. CASES OF MISTAKEN IDENTITY 23

   VI. DUAL AND TRIPLE BANSHEE HAUNTINGS 31

   VII. A SIMILAR CASE FROM SPAIN 39

  VIII. THE BANSHEE ON THE BATTLE-FIELD 50

   IX. THE BANSHEE AT SEA 55

   X. ALLEGED COUNTERPARTS OF THE BANSHEE 61

   XI. THE BANSHEE IN POETRY AND PROSE 72

   XII. THE BANSHEE IN SCOTLAND 81

  XIII. MY OWN EXPERIENCES WITH THE BANSHEE 96

     ADDENDA 102

THE BANSHEE

CHAPTER I

THE DEFINITION AND ORIGIN OF BANSHEES

In a country, such as Ireland, that is characterised by an arrestive and wildly beautiful scenery, it is not at all surprising to find something in the nature of a ghost harmonising with the general atmosphere and surroundings, and that something, apparently so natural to Ireland, is the Banshee.

The name Banshee seems to be a contraction of the Irish Bean Sidhe, which is interpreted by some writers on the subject "A Woman of the Faire Race," whilst by various other writers it is said to signify "The Lady of Death," "The Woman of Sorrow," "The Spirit of the Air," and "The Woman of the Barrow."

It is strictly a family ghost, and most authorities agree that it only haunts families of very ancient Irish lineage. Mr McAnnaly, for instance, remarks (in the chapter on Banshees in his "Irish Wonders"): "The Banshee attends only the old families, and though their descendants, through misfortune, may be brought down from high estate to ranks of peasant farmers, she never leaves nor forgets them till the last member has been gathered to his fathers in the churchyard."

A writer in the *Journal of the Cork Historical and Archæological Society* (Vol. V., No. 44, pp. 227-229) quotes an extract from a work entitled "Kerry Records," in which the following passage, relating to an elegiac poem written by Pierse Ferriter on Maurice Fitzgerald, occurs: "Aina, the Banshee who never wailed for any families who were not of Milesian blood, except the Geraldines, who became 'more Irish than the Irish themselves'; and in a footnote (see p. 229) it is only 'blood' that can have a Banshee. Business men nowadays have something as good as 'blood'— they have 'brains and brass,' by which they can compete with and enter into the oldest families in England and Ireland. Nothing, however, in an Irishman's estimation, can replace 'blue blood.'"

Sir Walter Scott, too, emphasises this point, and is even more specific and arbitrary. He confines the Banshee to families of pure Milesian stock, and declares it is never to be found attached to the descendants of the multitudinous English and Scotch settlers who have, from time to time, migrated to Ireland; nor even to the descendants of the Norman adventurers who accompanied Strongbow to the Green Isle in the twelfth century.

Lady Wilde[1] goes to the other extreme and allows considerable latitude. She affirms that the Banshee attaches itself not only to certain families of historic lineage, but also to persons gifted with song and music. For my own part I am in-

[1] "Ancient Legends, Mystic Charms and Superstitions of Ireland," by Lady Wilde.

clined to adopt a middle course; I do not believe that the Banshee would be deterred from haunting a family of historical fame and Milesian descent—such as the O'Neills or O'Donnells—simply because in that family was an occasional strain of Saxon or Norman blood, but, on the other hand, I do not think the Banshee would ever haunt a family that was not originally at least Celtic Irish—such, for instance, as the Fitz-Williams or Fitz-Warrens—although in that family there might happen to be periodic infusions of Milesian blood.

I disagree, *in toto*, with Lady Wilde's theory that, occasionally, the Banshee haunts a person who is extremely poetical and musical, simply because he happens to be thus talented. In my opinion, to be haunted by the Banshee one must belong to an Irish family that is, at least, a thousand years old; were it not so, we should assuredly find the Banshee haunting certain of the musical and poetical geniuses of every race all over the world—black and yellow, perhaps, no less than white—which certainly is not the case.

The Banshee, however, as Mr McAnnaly says, does, sometimes, travel; it travels when, and only when, it accompanies abroad one of the most ancient of the Irish families; otherwise it stays in Ireland, where, owing to the fact that there are few of the really old Irish families left, its demonstrations are becoming more and more rare.

It may, perhaps, be said that in Dublin, Cork, and other of the Irish towns one may still come across a very fair percentage of O's and Macs. That, undoubtedly, is true, but, at the same time, it must be borne in mind that these prefixes do not invariably denote the true Irishman, since many families yclept Thompson, Walker, and Smith, merely on the strength of having lived in Ireland for two or three generations, have adopted an Irish—and in some cases, even, a Celtic Irish name, relying upon their knowledge of a few Celtic words picked up from books, or from attending some of the numerous classes now being held in nearly all the big towns, and which are presided over by teachers who are also, for the most part, merely pseudo-Irish—to give colour to their claim. Such a pretence, however, does not deceive those who are really Irish, neither does it deceive the Banshee, and the latter, I am quite sure, would never be persuaded to follow the fortunes of any Anglo-Saxon, or Scotch, Dick, Tom, or Harry, no matter how clever and convincing their camouflage might be.

Once again, then, the Banshee confines itself solely to families of *bona-fide* ancient Irish descent. As to its origin, in spite of arbitrary assertions made by certain people, none of whom, by the way, are of Irish extraction—that no one knows. As a matter of fact the Banshee has a number of origins, for there is not one Banshee only—as so many people seem to think—but many; each clan possessing a Banshee of its own. The O'Donnell Banshee, for example, that is to say the Banshee attached to our branch of the clan, and to which I can testify from personal experience, is, I believe, very different in appearance, and in its manner of making itself known, from the Banshee of the O'Reardons, as described by Mr McAnnaly; whilst the Banshee of a certain branch of the O'Flahertys, according to this same authority, differs essentially from that of a branch of the O'Neills. Mr McAnnaly says the Banshee "is really a disembodied soul, that of one who, in life, was strongly attached to the family, or who had good reason to hate all its members." This definition, of course, may apply in some cases, but it certainly does not apply in all, and it is absurd to be dogmatic on a subject, concerning which it is quite impossible to obtain a very great deal of information. At the most, Mr McAnnaly can only speak with certainty of the comparatively few cases of Banshees that have come under his observation; there are, I think, scores of which he has never even heard. I myself know of several Banshee hauntings in which the phantom certainly cannot be that of any member of the human race; its features and proportions absolutely negative such a possibility, and I should have no hesitation in affirming that, in these cases, the phantom is what is commonly known as an elemental, or what I have termed in previous of my works, a neutrarian, that is a spirit that has never inhabited any material body, and which belongs to a species entirely distinct from man. On the other hand, several cases of Banshee hauntings I have come across undoubtedly admit the possibility of the phantom being that of a woman belonging to the human race, albeit to a very ancient and long since obsolete section of it; whilst a few, only, allow of the probability of the phantom being that of a woman, also human, but belonging to a very much later date.

Certainly, as Mr McAnnaly stated, Banshees may be divided into two main classes, the Friendly Banshees and the Hateful Banshees; the former exhibiting sorrow on their advent, and the latter, exultation. But these classes are capable of almost endless sub-division; the only feature they possess in common being a vague something that strongly suggests the feminine sex. In most cases the cause of the hauntings can only be a matter of conjecture. Affection or crime may account for some, but, for the origin of others, I believe one must look in a totally different direction. For instance, one might, perhaps, see some solution in sorcery and witchcraft, since there must be many families, who, in bygone days, dabbled in those pursuits, that are now Banshee ridden.

Or, again, granted there is some truth in the theory of Atlantis, the theory that a whole continent was submerged owing to the wickedness of its inhabitants, who were all more or less adepts in necromancy—the most ancient of the Irish, the so-called Milesian clans who are known to have practised sorcery, might well be identical with the survivors of that great cataclysm, and have brought with them to the Green Island spirits which have stuck to their descendants ever since.

I think one may dismiss Mr C. W. Leadbeater's[2] and other writers' (of the same would-be authoritative order) assertion that family ghosts may be either a thought-form or an unusually vivid impression in the astral light, as absurd. Spiritualists and others, who blindly reverence highfalutin phraseology, however empty it may be, might be satisfied with such an explanation, but not so those who have had actual experience with the ghost in question.

Whatever else the Banshee may, or may not be, it is most certainly a denizen of a world quite distinct from ours; it is, besides, a being that has prophetic powers (which would not be the case if it were a mere thought-form or impression), and it is by no means a mere automaton.

---

[2] "The Astral Plane," p. 106.

Some Banshees represent very beautiful women—women with long, luxuriant tresses, either of raven black, or burnished copper, or brilliant gold, and whose star-like eyes, full of tender pity, are either dark and tearful, or of the most exquisite blue or grey; some, again, are haggish, wild, dishevelled-looking creatures, whose appearance suggests the utmost squalor, foulness, and despair; whilst a few, fortunately, I think, only a few, take the form of something that is wholly diabolical, and frightful, and terrifying in the extreme.

As a rule, however, the Banshee is not seen, it is only heard, and it announces its advent in a variety of ways; sometimes by groaning, sometimes by wailing, and sometimes by uttering the most blood-curdling of screams, which I can only liken to the screams a woman might make if she were being done to death in a very cruel and violent manner. Occasionally I have heard of Banshees clapping their hands, and tapping and scratching at walls and window-panes, and, not infrequently, I have heard of them signalling their arrival by terrific crashes and thumps. Also, I have met with the Banshee that simply chuckles—a low, short, but terribly expressive chuckle, that makes ten times more impression on the mind of the hearer than any other ghostly sound he has heard, and which no lapse of time is ever able to efface from his memory.

I, for one, have heard the sound, and as I sit here penning these lines, I fancy I can hear it again—a Satanic chuckle, a chuckle full of mockery, as if made by one who was in the full knowledge of coming events, of events that would present an extremely unpleasant surprise. And, in my case, the unpleasant surprise came. I have always been a believer in a spirit world—in the unknown—but had I been ever so sceptical previously, after hearing that chuckle, I am quite sure I should have been converted.

In concluding this chapter I must refer once again to Mr McAnnaly, who, in his "Irish Wonders," records a very remarkable instance of a number of Banshees manifesting themselves simultaneously. He says that the demonstrations occurred before the death of a member of the Galway O'Flahertys "some years ago."[3] The doomed one, he states, was a lady of the most unusual piety, who, though ill at the time, was not thought to be seriously ill. Indeed, she got so much better that several of her acquaintances came to her room to enliven her convalescence, and it was when they were there, all talking together merrily, that singing was suddenly heard, apparently outside the window. They listened, and could distinctly hear a choir of very sweet voices singing some extraordinarily plaintive air, which made them turn pale and look at one another apprehensively, for they all felt intuitively it was a chorus of Banshees. Nor were their surmises incorrect, for the patient unexpectedly developed pleurisy, and died within a few days, the same choir of spirit voices being again heard at the moment of physical dissolution.

But as Mr McAnnaly states, the ill-fated lady was of singular purity, which doubtless explains the reason why, in my researches, I have never come across a parallel case.

---

[3] This book was published in 1888.

CHAPTER II

SOME HISTORICAL BANSHEES

Amongst the most popular cases of Banshee haunting both published and unpublished is that related by Ann, Lady Fanshawe, in her Memoirs. It seems that Lady Fanshawe experienced this haunting when on a visit to Lady Honora O'Brien, daughter of Henry, fifth Earl of Thomond[4], who was then, in all probability, residing at the ancient castle of Lemaneagh, near Lake Inchiquin, about thirty miles north-west of Limerick. Retiring to rest somewhat early the first night of her sojourn there, she was awakened at about one o'clock by the sound of a voice, and, drawing aside the hangings of the bed, she perceived, looking in through the window at her, the face of a woman. The moonlight being very strong and fully focussed on it, she could see every feature with startling distinctness; but at the same time her attention was apparently riveted on the extraordinary pallor of the cheeks and the intense redness of the hair. Then, to quote her own words, the apparition "spake loud, and in a tone I never heard, thrice 'Ahone,' and then with a sigh, more like wind than breath, she vanished, and to me her body looked more like a thick cloud than substance.

"I was so much affrighted that my hair stood on end, and my night clothes fell off. I pulled and pinched your father, who never awaked during this disorder I was in, but at last was much surprised to find me in this fright, and more when I related the story and showed him the window opened; but he entertained me with telling how much more these apparitions were usual in that country than in England."

The following morning Lady Honora, who did not appear to have been to bed, informed Lady Fanshawe that a cousin of hers had died in the house at about two o'clock in the morning; and expressed a hope that Lady Fanshawe had not been subjected to any disturbances.

"When any die of this family," she said by way of explanation, "there is the shape of a woman appears in this window every night until they be dead."

She went on to add that the apparition was believed to be that of a woman who, centuries before, had been seduced by the owner of the castle and murdered, her body being buried under the window of the room in which Lady Fanshawe had slept.

"But truly," she remarked, by way of apology, "I thought not of it when I

[4] In the Addenda at end of this volume will be found a genealogical tree showing descent of author from the Thomond O'Briens.

lodged you here."

Another well-known case of the Banshee is that relating to the O'Flahertys of Galway, reference being made to the case by Mr McAnnaly in his work entitled "Irish Wonders." In the days of much inter-clan fighting in Ireland, when the O'Neills frequently embarked on crusades against their alternate friends and enemies the O'Donnells, and the O'Rourks[5] embarked on similar crusades against the O'Donovans, it so happened that one night the chief of the O'Flahertys, arrayed in all the brilliance of a new suit of armour, and feeling more than usually cheerful and fit, marched out of his castle at the head of a numerous body of his retainers, who were all, like their chief, in good spirits, and talking and singing gaily. They had not proceeded far, however, when a sudden and quite inexplicable silence ensued—a silence that was abruptly broken by a series of agonising screams, that seemed to come from just over their heads. Instantly everyone was sobered, and naturally looked up, expecting to see something that would explain the extraordinary and terrifying disturbance; nothing, however, was to be seen, nothing but a vast expanse of cloudless sky, innumerable scintillating stars, and the moon which was shining forth in all the serene majesty of its zenith. Yet, despite the fact that nothing was visible, everyone felt a presence that was at once sorrowful and weird, and which one and all instinctively knew was the Banshee, the attendant spirit of the O'Flahertys, come to warn them of some approaching catastrophe.

The next night, when the chieftain and his followers were again sallying forth, the same thing happened, but, after that, nothing of a similar nature occurred for about a month. Then the wife of the O'Flaherty, during the absence of her husband on one of these foraging expeditions, had an experience. She had gone to bed one night and was restlessly tossing about, for, try how she would, she could not sleep, when she was suddenly terrified by a succession of the most awful shrieks, coming, apparently, from just beneath her window, and which sounded like the cries of some woman in the direst trouble or pain. She looked, but as she instinctively felt would be the case, she could see no one. She then knew that she had heard the Banshee; and on the morrow her forebodings were only too fully realised. With a fearful knowledge of its meaning, she saw a cavalcade, bearing in its midst a bier, slowly and sorrowfully wending its way towards the castle; and, needless to say, she did not require to be told that the foraging party had returned, and that the surviving warriors had brought back with them the lifeless and mutilated body of her husband.

The Kenealy Banshee furnishes yet another instance of this extremely fascinating and, up to the present, wholly enigmatical type of haunting. Dr Kenealy, the well-known Irish poet and author, resided in his earlier years in a wildly romantic and picturesque part of Ireland. Among his brothers was one, a mere child, whose sweet and gentle nature rendered him beloved by all, and it was a matter of the most excessive grief to the entire household, and, indeed, the whole neighbourhood, when this boy fell into a decline and his life was despaired of by the physicians. As time went on he grew weaker and weaker, until the moment at length

---

[5] In Addenda see tree showing descent of author from O'Rourks of Brefni.

arrived, when it was obvious that he could not possibly survive another twenty-four hours. At about noon, the room in which the patient lay was flooded with a stream of sunlight, which came pouring through the windows from the cloudless expanse of sky overhead. The weather, indeed, was so gorgeous that it seemed almost incredible that death could be hovering quite so near the house. One by one, members of the family stole into the chamber to take what each one felt might be a last look at the sick boy, whilst he was still alive. Presently the doctor arrived, and, as they were all discussing in hushed tones the condition of the poor wasted and doomed child, they one and all heard someone singing, apparently in the grounds, immediately beneath the window. The voice seemed to be that of a woman, but not a woman of this world. It was divinely soft and sweet, and charged with a pity and sorrow that no earthly being could ever have portrayed; and now loud, and now hushed, it continued for some minutes, and then seemed to die away gradually, like the ripple of a wavelet on some golden, sun-kissed strand, or the whispering of the wind, as it gently rustles its way through field after field of yellow, nodding corn.

"What a glorious voice!" one of the listeners exclaimed. "I've never heard anything to equal it."

"Very likely not," someone else whispered, "it's the Banshee!"

And so enthralled were they all by the singing, that it was only when the final note of the plaintive ditty had quite ceased, that they became aware that their beloved patient, unnoticed by them, had passed out. Indeed, it seemed as if the boy's soul, with the last whispering notes of the dirge, had joined the beautiful, pitying Banshee, to be escorted by it into the realms of the all-fearful, all-impatient Unknown. Dr Kenealy has commemorated this event in one of his poems.

The story of another haunting by the friendly Banshee is told in Kerry, in connection with a certain family that used to live there. According to my source of information the family consisted of a man (a gentleman farmer), his wife, their son, Terence, and a daughter, Norah.

Norah, an Irish beauty of the dark type, had black hair and blue eyes; and possessing numerous admirers, favoured none of them so much as a certain Michael O'Lernahan. Now Michael did not stand very well in the graces of either of Norah's parents, but Terence liked him, and he was reputed to be rich—that is to say rich for that part of Ireland. Accordingly, he was invited pretty freely to the farm, and no obstacles were placed in his way. On the contrary, he was given more than a fair amount of encouragement.

At last, as had been long anticipated, he proposed and Norah accepted him; but no sooner was her troth plighted than they both heard, just over their heads, a low, despairing wail, as of a woman in the very greatest distress and anguish.

Though they were much alarmed at the time, being positive that the sounds proceeded from no human being, neither of them seems to have regarded the phenomenon in the shape of a warning, and both continued their love-making as if the incident had never occurred. A few weeks later, however, Norah noticed a sudden change in her lover; he was colder and more distant, and, whilst he was with her, she invariably found him preoccupied. At last the blow fell. He failed to present himself at the house one evening, though he was expected as usual, and, as no explanation was forthcoming the following morning, nor on any of the succeeding days, inquiries were made by the parents, which elicited the fact that he had become engaged to another girl, and that the girl's home was but a few minutes' walk from the farm.

This proved too much for Norah; although, apparently, neither unusually sensitive nor particularly highly strung, she fell ill, and shortly afterwards died of a broken heart. It was not until the night before she died, however, that the Banshee paid her a second visit. She was lying on a couch in the parlour of the farmhouse, with her mother sitting beside her, when a noise was heard that sounded like leaves beating gently against the window-frames, and, almost directly afterwards, came the sound of singing, loud, and full of intense sorrow and compassion; and, obviously, that of a woman.

"'Tis the Banshee," the mother whispered, immediately crossing herself, and, at the same time, bursting into tears.

"The Banshee," Norah repeated. "Sure I hear nothing but that tapping at the window and the wind which seems all of a sudden to have risen."

But the mother made no response. She only sat with her face buried in her hands, sobbing bitterly and muttering to herself, "Banshee! Banshee!"

Presently, the singing having ceased, the old woman got up and dried her tears. Her anxiety, however, was not allayed; all through the night she could still be heard, every now and again, crying quietly and whispering to herself "'Twas the Banshee! Banshee!"; and in the morning Norah, suddenly growing alarmingly ill, passed away before medical assistance could be summoned.

A case of Banshee haunting that is somewhat unusually pathetic was once related to me in connection with a Dublin branch of the once powerful clan of McGrath.

It took place in the fifties, and the family, consisting of a young widow and two children, Isa and David, at that time occupied an old, rambling house, not five minutes' walk from Stephen's Green. Isa seems to have been the mother's favourite—she was undoubtedly a very pretty and attractive child—and David, possibly on account of his pronounced likeness to his father, with whom it was an open secret that Mrs McGrath had never got on at all well, to have received rather more than his fair share of scolding. This, of course, may or may not have been true. It is certain that he was left very much to himself, and, all alone, in a big, empty room at the top of the house, was forced to amuse himself as he best could. Occasionally one of the servants, inspired by a fellow-feeling—for the lot of servants in those days, especially when serving under such severe and exacting mistresses as Mrs McGrath, was none too rosy—used to look in to see how he was getting on and bring him a toy, bought out of her own meagre savings; and, once now and again, Isa, clad in some costly new frock, just popped her head in at the door, either to bring him some message from her mother, or merely to call out "Hullo!" Otherwise he saw no one; at least no one belonging to this earth; he only saw, he affirmed, at times, strange-looking people who simply stood and stared at him without speaking, people who the servants—girls from Limerick and the west country—assured him were either fairies or ghosts.

One day Isa, who had been sent upstairs to tell David to go to his bedroom to tidy himself, as he was wanted immediately in the drawing-room, found him in a great state of excitement.

"I've seen such a beautiful lady,"[6] he exclaimed, "and she wasn't a bit cross. She came and stood by the window and looked as if she wanted to play with me, only I daren't ask her. Do you think she will come again?"

"How can I tell? I expect you've been dreaming as usual," Isa laughed. "What was she like?"

"Oh, tall, much taller than mother," David replied, "with very, very blue eyes and kind of reddish-gold hair that wasn't all screwed up on her head, but was hanging in curls on her shoulders. She had very white hands which were clasped in front of her, and a bright green dress. I didn't see her come or go, but she was here for a long time, quite ten minutes."

"It's another of your fancies, David," Isa laughed again. "But come along, make haste, or mother will be angry."

A few minutes later, David, looking very shy and awkward, was in the drawing-room being introduced to a gentleman who, he was informed, was his future papa.

David seems to have taken a strong dislike to him from the very first, and to have foreseen in the coming alliance nothing but trouble and misery for himself. Nor were his apprehensions without foundation, for, directly after the marriage took place, he became subjected to the very strictest discipline. Morning and afternoon alike he was kept hard at his books, and any slowness or inability to master a lesson was treated as idleness and punished accordingly. The moments he had to himself in his beloved nursery now became few and far between, for, directly he had finished his evening preparation, he was given his supper and packed off to bed.

The one or two servants who had befriended him, unable to tolerate the new regime, gave notice and left, and there was soon no one in the house who showed any compassion whatever for the poor lonely boy.

Things went on in this fashion for some weeks, and then a day came, when he really felt it impossible to go on living any longer.

He had been generally run down for some weeks, and this, coupled with the fact that he was utterly broken in spirit, rendered his task of learning a wellnigh impossibility. It was in vain he pleaded, however; his entreaties were only taken for excuses; and, when, in an unguarded moment, he let slip some sort of reference to unkind treatment, he was at once accused of rudeness by his mother and, at her request, summarily castigated.

[6] As a rule the Banshee is neither heard nor seen by the person whose death it predicts. There are, however, some notable exceptions.

The limit of his tribulation had been reached. That night he was sent to bed, as usual, immediately after supper, and Isa, who happened to pass by his room an hour or so afterwards, was greatly astonished at hearing him seemingly engaged in conversation. Peeping slyly in at the door, in order to find out with whom he was talking, she saw him sitting up in bed, apparently addressing space, or the moonbeams, which, pouring in at the window, fell directly on him.

"What are you doing?" she asked, "and why aren't you asleep?"

The moment she spoke he looked round and, in tones of the greatest disappointment, said:

"Oh, dear, she's gone. You've frightened her away."

"Frightened her away! Why, what rubbish!" Isa exclaimed. "Lie down at once or I'll go and fetch mamma."

"It was my green lady," David went on, breathlessly, far too excited to pay any serious heed to Isa's threat. "My green lady, and she told me I should be no more lonely, that she was coming to fetch me some time to-night."

Isa laughed, and, telling him not to be so silly, but to go to sleep at once, she speedily withdrew and went downstairs to join her parents in the drawing-room.

That night, at about twelve, Isa was awakened by singing, loud and plaintive singing, in a woman's voice, apparently proceeding from the hall. Greatly alarmed she got up, and, on opening her door, perceived her parents and the servants, all in their night attire, huddled together on the landing, listening.

"Sure 'tis the Banshee," the cook at length whispered. "I heard my father spake about it when I was a child. She sings, says he, more beautifully than any grand lady, but sorrowful like, and only before a death."

"Before a death," Isa's mother stammered. "But who's going to die here? Why, we are all of us perfectly sound and well." As she spoke the singing ceased, there was an abrupt silence, and all slowly retired to their rooms.

Nothing further was heard during the night, but in the morning, when breakfast time came, there was no David; and a hue and cry being raised and a thorough search made, he was eventually discovered, drowned in a cistern in the roof.

CHAPTER III

THE MALEVOLENT BANSHEE

The Banshees dealt with in the last chapter may all be described as sympathetic or friendly Banshees. I will now present to the reader a few equally authentic accounts of malevolent or unfriendly Banshees. Before doing so, however, I would like to call attention to the fact that, once when I was reading a paper on Banshees before the Irish Literary Society, in Hanover Square, a lady got up and, challenging my remark that not all Banshees were alike, tried to prove that I was wrong, on the assumption that all Banshees must be sad and beautiful because the Banshee in her family happened to be sad and beautiful, an argument, if argument it can be called, which, although it is a fairly common one, cannot, of course, be taken seriously.

Moreover, as I have already stated, there is abundant evidence to show that Banshees are of many and diverse kinds; and that no two appear to be exactly alike or to act in precisely the same fashion.

According to Mr McAnnaly, the malevolent Banshee is invariably "a horrible hag with ugly, distorted features; maledictions are written in every line of her wrinkled face, and her outstretched arms call down curses on the doomed member of the hated race."

Other writers, too, would seem more or less to encourage the idea that all malignant Banshees are cast in one mould and all beautiful Banshees in another, whereas from my own personal experiences I should say that Banshees, whether good or bad, are just as individual as any member of the family they haunt.

It is related of a certain ancient Mayo family that a chief of the race once made love to a very beautiful girl whom he betrayed and subsequently murdered. With her dying breath the girl cursed her murderer and swore she would haunt him and his for ever. Years rolled by; the cruel deceiver married, and, with the passing away of all who knew him in his youth, he came to be regarded as a model of absolute propriety and rectitude. Hence it was in these circumstances that he was sitting one night before a big blazing fire in the hall of his castle, outwardly happy enough and surrounded by his sons and daughters, when loud shrieks of exultation were heard coming, it seemed, from someone who was standing on the path close to the castle walls. All rushed out to see who it was, but no one was there, and the grounds, as far as the eye could reach, were absolutely deserted.

Later on, however, some little time after the household had retired to rest, the same demoniacal disturbances took place; peal after peal of wild, malicious laughter rang out, followed by a discordant moaning and screaming. This time the aged chieftain did not accompany the rest of the household in their search for the originator of the disturbances. Possibly, in that discordant moaning and screaming he fancied he could detect the voice of the murdered girl; and, possibly, accepting the manifestation as a death-warning, he was not surprised on the following day, when he was waylaid out of doors and brutally done to death by one of his followers.

Needless to say, perhaps, the haunting of this Banshee still continues, the same phenomena occurring at least once to every generation of the family, before the death of one of its members. Happily, however, the haunting now does not necessarily precede a violent death, and in this respect, though in this respect only, differs from the original.

Another haunting by this same species of Banshee was brought to my notice the last time I was in Ireland. I happened to be visiting a certain relative of mine, at that date residing in Black Rock, and from her I learned the following, which now appears in print for the first time.

About the middle of the last century, when my relative was in her teens, some friends of hers, the O'D.'s, were living in a big old-fashioned country house, somewhere between Ballinanty and Hospital in the County of Limerick. The family consisted of Mr O'D., who had been something in India in his youth and was now very much of a recluse, though much esteemed locally on account of his extreme piety and good-heartedness; Mrs O'D., who, despite her grey hair and wrinkled countenance, still retained traces of more than ordinary good looks; Wilfred, a handsome but decidedly headstrong young man of between twenty-five and thirty; and Ellen, a blue-eyed, golden-haired girl of the true Milesian type of Irish beauty.

My relative was on terms of the greatest intimacy with the whole family, but especially with the two younger folk, and it was generally expected that she and Wilfred would make what is vulgarly termed a "match of it." Indeed, the first of the ghostly happenings that she experienced in connection with the O'D.'s actually occurred the very day Wilfred took the long-anticipated step and proposed to her.

It seems that my relative was out for a walk one afternoon with Ellen and Wilfred, when the latter, taking advantage of his sister's sudden fancy for going on ahead to look for dog-roses, passionately declared his love, and, apparently, did not declare it in vain. The trio, then, in more or less exalted spirits — for my relative had of course let Ellen into the secret — walked home together, and as they were passing through a big wooden gateway into the garden at the rear of the O'D.'s house, they perceived a tall, spare woman, with her back towards them, digging away furiously.

"Hullo," Wilfred exclaimed, "who's that?"

"I don't know," Ellen replied. "It's certainly not Mary" (Mary was the old cook who, like many of the servants of that period, did not confine her labour to the culinary art, but performed all kinds of odd jobs as well), "nor anyone from the farm.

But what on earth does she think she's doing? Hey, there!" and Ellen, raising her naturally sweet and musical voice, gave a little shout.

The woman instantly turned round, and the trio received a most violent shock. The light was fading, for it was late in the afternoon, but what little there was seemed to be entirely concentrated on the visage before them, making it appear luminous. It was a broad face with very pronounced cheek-bones; a large mouth, the thin lips of which were fixed in a dreadful and mocking leer; and very pale, obliquely set eyes that glowed banefully as they met the gaze of the three now appalled spectators.

For some seconds the evil-looking creature stood in dead silence, apparently gloating over the discomposure her appearance had produced, and, then, suddenly shouldering her spade, she walked slowly away, turning round every now and again to cast the same malevolent gleeful look at them, until she came to the hedge that separated the garden from a long disused stone quarry, when she seemed suddenly to fade away in the now very uncertain twilight, and disappear.

For some moments no one spoke or stirred, but continued gazing after her in a kind of paralysed astonishment. Wilfred was the first to break the silence.

"What an awful looking hag," he exclaimed. "Where's she gone?"

Ellen whistled. "Ask another," she said. "There's nowhere she could have gone excepting into the quarry, and my only hope is that she is lying at the bottom of it with a broken neck, for I certainly never wish to see her again. But come, let's be moving on, I'm chilly."

They started off, but had only proceeded a few yards, when, apparently from the direction of the quarry, came a peal of laughter, so mocking and malignant and altogether evil, that all three involuntarily quickened their steps, and, at the same time, refrained from speaking, until they had reached the house, which they hastily entered, securely closing the door behind them. They then went straight to Mr O'D. and asked him who the old woman was whom they had just seen.

"What was she like?" he queried. "I haven't authorised anyone but Mary to go into the garden."

"It certainly wasn't Mary," Ellen responded quickly. "It was some hideous old crone who was digging away like anything. On our approach she left off and gave us the most diabolical look I have ever seen. Then she went away and seemed to vanish in the hedge by the quarry. We afterwards heard her give the most appalling and intensely evil laugh that you can imagine. Whoever is she?"

"I can't think," Mr O'D. replied, looking somewhat unusually pale. "It is no one whom I know. Very possibly she was a tramp or gipsy. We must take care to keep all the doors locked. Whatever you do, don't mention a word about her to your mother or to Mary—they are both nervous and very easily frightened."

All three promised, and the matter was then allowed to drop, but my relative, who returned home before it got quite dark, subsequently learned that that night, some time after the O'D. household had all retired to rest, peal after peal of the same infernal mocking laughter was heard, just under the windows, first of all in the front of the house, and then in the rear; and that, on the morrow, came the news that the business concern in which most of Mr O'D.'s money was invested had gone smash and the family were practically penniless.

The house now was in imminent danger of being sold, and many people thought that it was merely to avert this catastrophe and to enable her parents to keep a roof over their heads that Ellen accepted the attentions of a very vulgar parvenu (an Englishman) in Limerick, and eventually married him. Where there is no love, however, there is never any happiness, and where there is not even "liking," there is very often hate; and in Ellen's case hate there was without any doubt. Barely able, even from the first, to tolerate her husband (his favourite trick was to make love to her in public and almost in the same breath bully her—also in public), she eventually grew to loathe him, and at last, unable to endure his hated presence any longer, she eloped with an officer who was stationed in the neighbourhood. The night before Ellen took this step, my relative and Wilfred (the latter was escorting his fiancée home after a pleasant evening spent in her company) again heard the malevolent laughter, which (although they could see no one) pursued them for some distance along the moonlit lanes and across the common leading to the spot where my relative lived. After this the laughter was not heard again for two years, but at the end of that period my relative had another experience of the phenomena.

She was again spending the evening with the O'D.'s, and, on this occasion, she was discussing with Mr and Mrs O'D. the advent of Wilfred, who was expected to arrive home from the West Indies any time within the next few days. My relative was not unnaturally interested, as it had been arranged that she and Wilfred should marry, as soon as possible after his arrival in Ireland. They were all three—Mr and Mrs O'D. and my relative—engaged in animated conversation (the old people had unexpectedly come into a little money, and that, too, had considerably contributed to their cheerfulness), when Mrs O'D., fancying she heard someone calling to her from the garden, got up and went to the window.

"Harry," she exclaimed, still looking out and apparently unable to remove her gaze, "do come. There's the most awful old woman in the garden, staring hard at me. Quick, both of you. She's perfectly horrible; she frightens me."

My relative and Mr O'D. at once sprang up and hastened to her side, and, there, they saw, gazing up at them, the pallor of its cheeks intensified by a stray moonbeam which seemed to be concentrated solely on it, a face which my relative recognised immediately as that of the woman she had seen, two years ago, digging in the garden. The old hag seemed to remember my relative, too, for, as their glances met, a gleam of recognition crept into her light eyes, and, a moment later, gave way to an expression of such diabolical hate that my relative involuntarily caught hold of Mr O'D. for protection. Evidently noting this action the creature leered horribly, and then, drawing a kind of shawl or hood tightly over its head, moved away with a kind of gliding motion, vanishing round an angle of the wall.

Mr O'D. at once went out into the garden, but, after a few minutes, returned, declaring that, although he had searched in every direction, not a trace of their sinister-looking visitor could he see anywhere. He had hardly, however, finished speaking, when, apparently from close to the house, came several peals of the most hellish laughter, that terminated in one loud, prolonged wail, unmistakably ominous and menacing.

"Oh, Harry," Mrs O'D. exclaimed, on the verge of fainting, "what can be the meaning of it? That was surely no living woman."

"No," Mr O'D. replied slowly, "it was the Banshee. As you know, the O'D. Banshee, for some reason or another, possesses an inveterate hatred of my family, and we must prepare again for some evil tidings. But," he went on, steadying his voice with an effort, "with God's grace we must face it, for whatever happens it is His Divine will."

A few days later my relative, as may be imagined, was immeasurably shocked to hear that Mr O'D. had been sent word that Wilfred was dead. He had, it appeared, been stricken down with fever, supposed to have been caught from one of his fellow-passengers, and had died on the very day that he should have landed, on the very day, in fact (as it was afterwards ascertained from a comparison of dates), upon which his parents and fiancée, together, had heard and seen the Banshee.

Soon after this unhappy event my relative left the neighbourhood and went to live with some friends near Dublin, and though, from time to time, she corresponded with the O'D.'s, she never again heard anything of their Banshee.

This same relative of mine, whom I will now call Miss S— — (she never married), was acquainted with two old maiden ladies named O'Rorke who, many years ago, lived in a semi-detached house close to Lower Merrion Street. Miss S— — did not know to what branch of the O'Rorkes they belonged, for they were very reticent with regard to their family history, but she believed they originally came from the south-west and were distantly connected with some of her own people.

With regard to their house, there certainly was something peculiar, since in it was one room that was invariably kept locked, and in connection with this room it was said there existed a mystery of the most frightful and harrowing description.

My relative often had it on the tip of her tongue to refer to the room, just to see what effect it would have on the two old ladies, but she could never quite sum up the courage to do so. One afternoon, however, when she was calling on them, the subject was brought to their notice in a very startling manner.

The elder of the two sisters, Miss Georgina, who was presiding at the tea table, had just handed Miss S— — a cup of tea and was about to pour out another for herself, when into the room, with her cap all awry and her eyes bulging, rushed one of the servants.

"Good gracious!" Miss Georgina exclaimed, "whatever's the matter, Bridget?"

"Matter!" Bridget retorted, in a brogue which I will not attempt to imitate. "Why, someone's got into that room you always keep locked and is making the devil of a noise, enough to raise all the Saints in Heaven. Norah" (Norah was the cook) "and I both heard it—a groaning, and a chuckling, and a scratching, as if the cratur was tearing up the boards and breaking all the furniture, and all the while keening and laughing. For the love of Heaven, ladies, come and hear it for yourselves. Such goings on! Ochone! Ochone!"

Both ladies, Miss S— — said, turned deadly pale, and Miss Harriet, the younger sister, was on the brink of tears.

"Where is cook?" Miss Georgina, who was by far the stronger minded of the two, suddenly said, addressing Bridget. "If she is upstairs, tell her to come down at once. Miss Harriet and I will go and see what the noise is that you complain about upstairs. There really is no need to make all this disturbance"—here she assumed an air of the utmost severity—"it's sure to be either mice or rats."

"Mice or rats!" Bridget echoed. "I'm sorry for the mice and rats as make all those noises. 'Tis some evil spirit, sure, and Norah is of the same mind," and with those parting words she slammed the door behind her.

The sisters, then, begging to be excused for a few minutes, left the room, and returned shortly afterwards looking terribly white and distressed.

"I am sure you must think all this very odd," Miss Georgina observed with as great a degree of unconcern as she could assume, "and I feel we owe you an explanation, but I must beg you will not repeat a word of what we tell you to anyone else."

Miss S— — promised she would not, and then composed herself to listen.

"We have in our family," Miss O'Rorke began, "a most unpleasant attachment; in other words, a most unpleasant Banshee. Being Irish, you will not laugh, of course, as many English people do, at what I say. You know as well as I do, perhaps, that many of the really ancient Irish families possess Banshees."

Miss S— — nodded. "We have one ourselves," she remarked, "but pray go on. I am intensely interested."

"Well, unlike most of the Banshees," Miss Georgina continued, "ours is appallingly ugly and malevolent; so frightful, indeed, that to see it, even, is sometimes fatal. One of our great-great-uncles, for instance, to whom it once appeared, is reported to have died from shock; a similar fate overtaking another of our ancestors, who also saw it. Fortunately, it seems to have a strong attraction in the shape of an old gold ring which has been in the possession of the family from time immemorial. Both ancestors I have referred to are alleged to have been wearing this ring at the time the Banshee appeared to them, and it is said to strictly confine its manifestations to the immediate vicinity of that article. That is why our parents always kept the ring strictly isolated, in a locked room, the key of which was never, for a moment, allowed to be out of their possession. And we have strenuously followed their example. That is the explanation of the mystery you have doubtless heard about, for I believe—thanks to the servants—it has become the gossip of half Dublin."

"And the noise Bridget referred to," Miss S— — ventured to remark, somewhat timidly, "was that the Banshee?"

Miss Georgina nodded.

"I fear it was," she observed solemnly, "and that we shall shortly hear of a relative's death or grave catastrophe to some member of the family; probably, a cousin of ours in County Galway, who has been ill for some weeks, is dying."

She was partly right, although the latter surmise was not correct. Within a few days of the Banshee's visit a member of the family died, but it was not the sick cousin, it was Miss Georgina's own sister, Harriet!

CHAPTER IV

THE BANSHEE ABROAD

As I have remarked in a previous chapter, the Banshee to-day is heard more often abroad than in Ireland. It follows the fortunes of the true old Milesian Irishman—the real O and Mc, none of your adulterated O'Walters or O'Cassons—everywhere, even to the Poles.

Lady Wilde, in her "Ancient Legends, Mystic Charms and Superstitions of Ireland," quotes the case of a Banshee haunting that was experienced by a branch of the Clan O'Grady that had settled in Canada.

The spot chosen by this family for their residence was singularly wild and isolated, and one night at two o'clock, when they were all in bed, they were aroused by a loud cry, coming, apparently, from just outside the house. Nothing intelligible was uttered, only a sound indicative of the greatest bitterness and sorrow, such as one might imagine a woman would give vent to, but only when in an agony of mind, almost beyond human understanding.

The effect produced by it was one of sublime terror, and all seemed to feel instinctively that the source from which it emanated was apart from this world and belonged wholly and solely to the Unknown. Nevertheless, from what Lady Wilde says, we are led to infer that an exhaustive search of the premises was made, resulting, as was expected, in complete failure to find any physical agency that could in any way account for the cry.

The following day the head of the household and his eldest son went boating on a lake near the house, and, although it was their intention to do so, did not return to dinner. Various members of the family were sent to look for them, but no trace of them was to be seen anywhere, and no solution to the mystery as to what had happened to them was forthcoming, till two o'clock that night, when, exactly twenty-four hours after the cry had been heard, some of the searchers returned, bearing with them the wet, bedraggled, and lifeless bodies of both father and son. Then, once again, the weird and ominous sound that had so startled them on the previous night was heard, and the sorrow-stricken family—that is to say, those who were left of it—agreeing now that the Banshee had indeed visited them, remembered that their beloved father, whom they had just lost, had often spoken of the Banshee, as having haunted their branch of the clan for countless generations.

Another case of Banshee haunting, that I have in mind, relates to a branch of the southern O'Neills that settled in Italy a good many years ago. It was told me in Paris by a Mrs Dempsey, who assured me she had been an eye-witness of the phenomena, and I now record it in print for the first time.

Mrs Dempsey, when staying once at an hotel in the north of Italy, noticed among the guests an elderly man, whose very marked features and intensely sad expression quickly attracted her attention. She observed that he kept entirely aloof from his fellow-guests, and that, every evening after dinner, he retired from the drawing-room, as soon as coffee had been handed round, and went outside and stood on the veranda overlooking the shore of the Adriatic.

She made inquiries as to his name and history, and was told that he was Count Fernando Asioli, a wealthy Florentine citizen, who, having but recently lost his wife, to whom he was devoted, naturally did not wish to join in the general conversation. Upon hearing this Mrs Dempsey was more than ever interested. It was not so very long since she, too, had lost her partner—a husband to whom she was much attached—and, consequently, it was in sympathetic mood that, seeing the Count go out, as usual, one evening, on to the veranda, she resolved to follow him, to try, if possible, to get into conversation with him.

With this end in view she was about to cross the threshold of the veranda, when, to her astonishment, she perceived the Count was not there alone. Standing by his side, with one hand laid caressingly on his shoulder, was a tall, slim girl, with masses of the most gorgeous red gold hair hanging loose and reaching to her waist. She was wearing an emerald green dress of some very filmy substance; but her arms and feet were bare, and stood out so clearly in the soft radiance of the moonbeams, that Mrs Dempsey, who was an artist and had studied on the Continent, noticed with a thrill that they equalled, if, indeed, they did not surpass in beauty, any she had ever come across either in Greek or Florentine sculpture.

Much perplexed as to who such a queerly attired visitor on such friendly terms with the Count could be, Mrs Dempsey remained for a second or two watching, and then, afraid lest she should attract their attention and so be caught, seemingly, in the act of spying, she withdrew.

The moment she got back again into the drawing-room, however, she made somewhat indignant inquiries of a lady who generally sat next to her at meals, as to the identity of the girl she had just seen standing beside the, said to be, heart-broken Count in an attitude of such close intimacy.

"A woman with the Count!" was the reply. "Surely not! Who can she be, and what was she like?"

Mrs Dempsey described the stranger in detail, but her friend, shaking her head, could only suggest that she was some new-comer, some guest who had arrived at the hotel, and gone on the veranda whilst they were at dinner. Feeling a little curious, however, Mrs Dempsey's friend walked towards the veranda, and, in a very short time, returned, looking somewhat puzzled.

"You must have been mistaken," she whispered, "there is no one with Count Asioli now, and, if anyone had come away, we should have seen them."

"I am quite sure I did see a woman there," Mrs Dempsey replied, "and only a minute or two ago; she must have got out somehow, although there is, apparently, no other way than through this room."

At this moment, the Count, entering the room, took a seat beside them; and the subject, of course, had to be dropped. The next night, however, the events of the preceding night were repeated. Mrs Dempsey followed the Count on to the veranda, saw the girl in green standing with her hand on his shoulder, came back and told her neighbour at meals, and the latter, on hastening to the veranda to look, once more returned declaring that the Count was alone. After this, a slight altercation took place between the two ladies, the one declaring her belief that it was all an optical illusion on the part of the other, and the other emphatically sticking to her story that she had actually seen the girl she had described.

They parted that night, both a little ruffled, though neither would admit it, and the following night, Mrs Dempsey, as soon as she saw the Count go on to the veranda, fetched her friend.

"Now," she said, "come with me and see for yourself."

The two ladies, accordingly, went to the veranda and, opening the door gently, peeped in.

"There she is," Mrs Dempsey whispered, "standing in just the same position."

The sound of her voice, though so low as to be scarcely heard even by the lady standing beside her, seemingly attracted the attention of both the girl and the Count, for they turned round simultaneously. Then Mrs Dempsey, whose gaze was solely concentrated on the girl, saw a face of almost indescribable beauty — possessing neatly chiselled, but by no means coldly classical features, long eyes of a marvellous blue, a smooth broad brow, and delicately and subtly moulded mouth; it was the face of a young girl, barely out of her teens, and it was filled with an expression of infinite sorrow and affection.

Mrs Dempsey was so enraptured that, to quote her own words, she "stood gazing at it in speechless awe and amazement," and might, perhaps, have been gazing at it still, had not the voice of the Count called her back to earth.

"I hope, ladies," he was saying, "that you do not see anything unusually disturbing in my appearance to-night, for I undoubtedly seem to be the object of your solicitude. May I ask why?"

Though he spoke quite politely, even the dullest could have seen that he was more than a little annoyed. Mrs Dempsey therefore hastened to reply.

"It is not you," she stammered out, "it is the lady — the lady you have with you. I — I fancied I knew her."

"The lady I have with me," the Count exclaimed, in accents of cold surprise. "Kindly explain what you mean?"

"Why the lady — —" Mrs Dempsey began, and then she glanced round.

The Count was standing in front of her — but he was quite alone. There was no vestige of a girl in green, nor of any other person on the veranda saving themselves, and immediately beneath it, at a distance of at least thirty feet, glimmered the white shingles of the silent and deserted—utterly deserted—seashore.

"She's gone," Mrs Dempsey cried, "but I'm positive I saw her—a lady in green standing beside you." Then, for the first time, she felt afraid, and trembled.

The Count, who had been observing her very closely, now advanced a step or two towards her, and in a very different tone said:

"Will you please describe the lady? Was she old or young, dark or fair?"

"Young and fair, very fair," Mrs Dempsey exclaimed. "But please come inside, for I've received something of a shock, and can, perhaps, talk to you better in the gaslight, with people near at hand whom I know are human beings."

He did as she requested, and became more and more interested as she proceeded with her description, interrupting her every now and again with questions. Was she sure the girl had blue eyes, he asked, and how could she tell what colour the eyes were by the light of the moon only; Mrs Dempsey's reply to which being that the girl's whole body seemed to be illuminated from within, in such a manner that every detail could be seen, almost, if not quite, as clearly as if she had been standing in the full glare of an electric light. At the conclusion of her narrative Mrs Dempsey was further questioned by the Count.

"Had she," he inquired, "ever been told that he was partly Irish, because," he added, on receiving a negative reply, "I am, and my real name is O'Neill, my great-great-grandfather having assumed the name of Asioli in order to come into some property when the family, which came from the south of Ireland, settled in Italy, many, many years ago. But what will, I am sure, be of considerable interest to you is the fact that this branch of the O'Neills, the branch to which I belong, is haunted by a Banshee, and that that Banshee has, I believe—since the description of it given me by various members of my family tallies with the description you have given me of the girl you saw standing by me—appeared to you. I would add that it never reveals itself, excepting when an O'Neill is about to die, and as I am quite the last of my line, I cannot conceive any reason for its having thus appeared three nights in succession, unless, of course, it is to predict my own end."

Mrs Dempsey was not long left in doubt. On the morrow the Count was summoned to Venice on urgent business, and on his way to the railway depôt he suddenly dropped down dead, the excitement and exertion having, so it was supposed, proved too much for his heart, which was known to be weak.

Said to be descended from the younger of the two sons of King Milesius, it certainly is not surprising that the O'Neills[7] should possess a Banshee—indeed, it would be surprising if they did not—but I have found it somewhat difficult to trace. However, according to Lady Wilde in her "Irish Wonders," p. 112, there is a room at Shane Castle which is strictly set aside for it.

The Banshee, Lady Wilde says, is very often seen in this apartment, sometimes appearing shrouded in a dark, mist-like mantle; and at other times as a very lovely young girl with long, red-gold hair, clad in a scarlet cloak and green kirtle, adorned with gold. Lady Wilde goes on to tell us no harm ever comes of the Ban-

[7] For further reference to the Banshee of the O'Neills see Addenda.

shee's visit, unless she is seen in the act of crying, when her wails may be taken as a certain sign that some member of the family will shortly die. Mr McAnnaly corroborates this by stating that on one occasion one of the O'Neills of Shane Castle heard the Banshee crying, just as he was about to set out on a journey, and perished soon afterwards, which is somewhat unusual, because in the majority of cases I have come across the Banshee does not manifest itself at all to the person whose death it predicts. A very old, probably the oldest, branch of the O'Neills now resides in Portugal, but up to the present I have not succeeded in obtaining any evidence to warrant the assumption that the Banshee haunting has been experienced in that country.

Indeed, the Banshee seems to be just as erratic and wayward as any daughter of Eve, for there is no consistency whatever in her movements. The very families one thinks she would haunt, she often studiously avoids, and not infrequently she concentrates her attention on those who are utterly obscure, albeit, always of *bona fide* Irish extraction.

CHAPTER V

CASES OF MISTAKEN IDENTITY

In previous chapters I have dealt exclusively with cases that are, without doubt, those of genuine Banshee haunting. I now propose to narrate a few cases which I will term cases of doubtful Banshee haunting—that is to say, cases of haunting which, although said to be Banshee, cannot, in view of the phenomena and circumstances, be thus designated with any degree of certainty.

To begin with I will recall the case relating to the R——s, a family living in Canada. Their house, a long, low, two-storied building, stood on a lonely spot on the road leading to Montreal, and a young lady, whom I will designate Miss Delane, was visiting them when the incidents I am about to narrate took place.

The weather had been more than commonly fine for that time of year, but at last the inevitable and unmistakable signs of a break had set in, and one evening black clouds gathered in the sky, the wind whistled ominously in the chimneys and savagely shook the many-coloured maple leaves, while, after a time, the moon, which had been hanging like a great red globe over the St Lawrence, became suddenly obscured, and big drops of rain came spluttering against the windows.

Miss Delane, who had been seized with a strange restlessness which she could not shake off, then went into the hall, and was about to speak to one of Major R——'s nieces, who was also on a visit there, when her attention was arrested by the sound of a heavy carriage lumbering along the high road, from the direction of Montreal, at a very great rate. It being now nearly ten o'clock, an hour when there was usually very little traffic, she was somewhat surprised, her astonishment increasing by leaps and bounds when she heard the wheels crunching on the gravel drive, and the carriage rapidly approaching the house.

"Surely, it is too late——" she began, but was cut short by the Major, who, abruptly pushing past her to the front door, just as the carriage drew up, swung it to, and, in trembling haste, locked, and barred, and bolted it.

Footsteps were then heard hurriedly ascending the steps to the front door, and immediately afterwards a series of loud rat-tat-tats, although, as everyone instantly remembered, there was no knocker on the door, the Major having had it removed many years ago, for a reason he either could not or would not explain.

Startled almost out of their senses by the noise, the whole household had in a few seconds assembled in the hall, and they now knelt, huddled together, whilst the Major in a voice which, despite the fact that it was raised to its highest pitch, could barely be heard above the furious and frenzied knocking, besought the Almighty to protect them.

As he continued praying the rat-tats gradually grew feebler and feebler, until they finally ceased, after which the footsteps were once again heard on the stone steps, this time descending, and the carriage drove away. It was not, however, until the reverberations of the wheels could no longer be heard that the Major rose from his knees. Then, bidding his household do likewise, he insisted that they should at once retire, without speaking a word, to their rooms; and forbade them ever to mention the matter to him again.

As soon as Miss Delane and the Major's nieces were in their bedroom—they shared a room between them—they ran to the window and looked out. The sky was quite clear now, and the moon was shining forth in all the splendour of its calm cold majesty; but the grounds and road beyond were quite deserted; not a vestige of any person or carriage could be seen anywhere, and, on the morrow, when they hastened downstairs and examined the gravel, there were no indications whatever of any wheels.

The day passed quite uneventfully, and once again it was night-time; the Major had read prayers as usual at about ten, and the household, also as usual, had retired to rest. Miss Delane, who was used to much later hours, found it difficult to compose herself to sleep so soon, but she had just managed to doze off, when she was aroused by her friend Ellen, the elder of the Major's two nieces, pulling violently at her bedclothes, and, on looking up, she perceived a tall figure, clad in what looked like nun's garments, walking across the room with long, stealthy strides. As she gazed at it in breathless astonishment, it suddenly paused and, turning its hooded head round, stared fixedly at Ellen, and then, moving on, seemed to melt into the wall. At all events, it had vanished, and there was nothing where it had been standing, saving moonlight.

For some minutes Ellen was too terrified to speak, but she at last called out to Miss Delane and implored her to come and get into her bed, as she no longer dared lie there by herself.

"Did you see the way it looked at me," she whispered, clutching hold of Miss Delane, and shuddering violently. "I don't think I shall ever get over it. We must leave here to-morrow. We must, we must," and she burst out crying.

As may be imagined, there was little sleep for either of the girls again that night, and it seemed to them as if the morning would never come; but, when at last it did come, they told Major R—— what had happened, and declared they really dared not spend another night in the house.

Though obviously distressed on hearing what they had to say, the Major did not press them to alter their decision and stay, but told them that to go, he thought, under the circumstances, was far the wisest and safest thing for them to do. An hour or so later, having finished their packing, they were all three taking a final stroll together in the garden, when they fancied they heard someone running after them down one of the sidewalks, and, turning round, they saw the figure that had disturbed them in the night, standing close behind them.

The sunlight falling directly on it revealed features now only too easily distinguishable of someone long since dead, but animated by a spirit that was wholly antagonistic and malicious, and as they shrank back terror-stricken, it stretched forth one of its long, bony arms and touched first Ellen and then her sister on the shoulder. It then veered round, and, moving away with the same peculiarly long and surreptitious strides, seemed suddenly to amalgamate with the shadows from the trees and disappear.

For some moments the girls were far too paralysed with fear to do other than remain where they were, trembling; but their faculties at length reasserting themselves, they made a sudden dash for the house, and ran at top speed till they reached it.

It was some weeks afterwards, however, and not till then, that Miss Delane, who was back again in her home in Ireland, received any explanation of the phenomena she had witnessed. It was given her by a friend of the R——s who happened to be visiting one of Miss Delane's relatives in Dublin.

"What you saw," this friend of the R——s said to Miss Delane, "was, I believe, the Banshee, which always manifests itself before the death of any member of the family. Sometimes it shrieks, like the shrieking of a woman who is being cruelly done to death, and sometimes it merely stares at or touches its victim on the shoulder with its skeleton hand. In either case its advent is fatal. Only," she added, "let me implore you never to breathe a word of this to the R——s, as they never mention their ghost to anyone."

Miss Delane, of course, promised, at the same time expressing a devout hope that the phenomena she had witnessed did not point to the illness or death of either of her friends; but in this she was doomed to the deepest disappointment, for within a few weeks of the date upon which the Banshee—if Banshee it really were—had appeared, she received tidings of the deaths of both Ellen and her sister (the former succumbing to an attack of some malignant fever, and the latter to an accident), and in addition heard that Major R—— had died also. As Major R—— would never discuss the subject of his family ghost with anyone at all, it is impossible to say whether he believed the haunting to be a Banshee haunting or not; but many, apparently, did believe it to be this type of haunting, and I must say I think they were wrong.

To begin with, the R——s were Anglo-Irish. Their connection with Ireland may have dated back a century or so, but they were certainly not of Milesian nor even Celtic Irish descent; and, for this reason alone, could not have acquired a Banshee haunting. Besides, the Banshee that we know does not appear, as the R——'s ghost appeared, attired in the vestments of a religious order; and the coach or hearse phantasm (which in the R——'s case preceded the manifestation of the supposed Banshee) is by no means an uncommon haunting;[8] and since it is more often than not accompanied by phenomena of the sepulchral type (the type witnessed by Miss Delane and the Major's nieces), it may be said to constitute in itself a peculiar form of family haunting which is not, of course, exclusively confined to

---

[8] See Addenda.

the Irish.

Hence I entirely dismiss the theory that the notorious R——'s ghost had any-thing at all to do with the Banshee. À propos of coaches, I am reminded of an inci-dent related by that past master of the weird, J. Sheridan Le Fanu, in a short story entitled "A Chapter in the History of a Tyrone Family." As it relates to that type of phantasm that is so often foolishly confused with the Banshee, I think I cannot do better than give a brief sketch of it.

Miss Richardson, a young Anglo-Irish girl, resided with her parents at Ash-town, Tyrone, and her elder sister, who had recently married a Mr Carew of Dub-lin, being expected with her husband on a visit, great preparations were on foot for their reception.

They were leaving Dublin by coach on the Monday morning, they had written to say, and hoped to arrive at Ashtown some time the following day. The morn-ing and afternoon passed, however, without any sign of the Carews, and when it got dark, and still they did not come, the Richardson family began to feel a trifle uneasy.

The night was fine, the sky cloudless, and the moon, when it at length rose, could not have been more brilliant. It was a still night, too, so still that not a leaf stirred, and so still that those on the qui vive, who were straining their ears to the utmost, must have caught the sound of an approaching vehicle on the high road, had there been one, when it was still at a distance of several miles. But no sound came, and when suppertime arrived, Mr Richardson, as was his wont, made a tour of the house, and carefully fastened the shutters and locked the doors. Still the family listened, and still they could hear nothing, nothing, either near to, or far away.

It was now midnight, but no one went to bed, for all were buoyed up with the desperate hope that something must at last happen—either, the Carews them-selves would suddenly turn up, or a messenger with a letter explaining the delay.

Neither eventuality, however, came to pass, and nothing occurred until Miss Richardson, who had, for the moment, allowed her mind to dwell on an entirely different topic, gave a start. Her heart beat loud, and she held her breath! She heard carriage wheels. Yes, without a doubt, she heard wheels—the wheels of a coach or carriage, and they were getting more and more distinct. But she remained silent. She had been rebuked once or twice for giving a false alarm—she would now let someone else speak first. In the meantime, on and on came the wheels, stopping for a moment whilst the iron gate at the entrance to the drive was swung open on its rusty hinges; then on and on again, louder, louder and louder, till all could distinguish, amid the barking of the dogs, the sound of scattered gravel and the crackling and swishing of the whip. There was no doubt about it now, and with joyous cries of "It is them! They have come at last," a regular stampede was made for the hall door, parents and sister, servants and dogs, vying with one another to see who could get there first. But, lo and behold, when the door was opened, and they stepped out, there was no sign of a coach or carriage anywhere; nothing was to be seen but the broad gravel drive and lawn beyond, alight with moonbeams and peopled with queer shadows, but absolutely silent, with a silence that suggested a churchyard.

The whole household now looked at one another with white and puzzled faces; they began to be afraid; whilst the dogs, running about, and sniffing, and whining, were obviously ill at ease and afraid, too.

At last a kind of panic set in, and all made a rush for the house, taking care, when once inside, to shut the door with even greater haste than they had displayed in opening it. The family then retired to rest, but not to sleep, and early the next morning they received news that fully confirmed their suspicions. Mrs Carew had been taken ill with fever on Monday, while preparations for the departure were being made, and had passed away, probably at the very moment when the Richardsons, hearing the phantom coach and mistaking it for a real one, had opened their hall door to welcome her.

That is the gist of the incident as related by Mr Le Fanu, and I have quoted it merely to show how a case of this kind, especially when it happens in Ireland, and to a family that has for some time been associated with Ireland, may sometimes be mistaken for a genuine Banshee haunting, although, of course, there is no reason whatever to suppose that Mr Le Fanu himself laboured under any delusion with regard to it, or intended to convey to his readers an impression of the haunting that the circumstances did not warrant. He merely states it as a case of the supernatural without attempting to consign it to any special category.

Lady Wilde in her "Ancient Cures, Charms and Usages of Ireland," pp. 163, 164, quotes another case of coach haunting in Ireland, a very terrible one; while in a book entitled "Rambles in Northumberland," by the same author, we are informed, "when the death-hearse, drawn by headless horses and driven by a headless driver, is seen about midnight proceeding rapidly, but without noise, towards the churchyard, the death of some considerable personage in the parish is sure to happen at no distant period." Also, there is a phantom of this description that is occasionally seen on the road near Langley in Durham, and my relatives, the Vizes[9] of Limerick—atleast, so my grandmother, *née* Sally Vize, used to say—are haunted by a phantom coach too; indeed, there seems to be no end to this kind of haunting, which is always either very picturesque or very terrifying, and sometimes both picturesque and terrifying.

At the same time, although intensely interesting, no doubt, the phantom coach is not essentially Irish, and not in any way connected with the Banshee.

As an example of the extreme anxiety of some people to be thought to be of ancient Irish extraction and to have a Banshee, I might refer to an incident in connection with Mrs Elizabeth Sheridan, which is recorded in footnotes on pages 32 and 33 of "The Memoirs of the Life and Writings of Mrs Frances Sheridan," compiled by her granddaughter, Miss Alicia Lefanu, and published in 1824, and quote from it the following:

"Like many Irish ladies who resided during the early part of life in the country, Miss Elizabeth Sheridan was a firm believer

[9] See Addenda.

in the Banshi, a female dæmon, attached to ancient Irish families. She seriously maintained that the Banshi of the Sheridan family was heard wailing beneath the windows of Quilca before the news arrived of Mrs Frances Sheridan's death at Blois, thus affording them a preternatural intimation of the impending melancholy event. A niece of Miss Sheridan's made her very angry by observing that as Miss Frances Sheridan was by birth a Chamberlaine, a family of English extraction, she had no right to the guardianship of an Irish fairy, and that, therefore, the Banshi must have made a mistake."

Now I certainly agree with Miss Sheridan's niece in doubting that the cry heard before Mrs Frances Sheridan's death was that of the real Banshee; but I do not doubt it because Mrs Frances Sheridan was of English extraction, for the Banshee has frequently been heard before the death of a wife whose husband was one of an ancient Irish clan—even though the wife had no Irish blood in her at all, but I doubt it because the husband of Mrs Frances Sheridan was one of a family who, not being of really ancient Irish descent, does not, in my opinion, possess a Banshee.

In "Personal Sketches of his Own Times," by Sir Jonah Barrington, we find (pp. 152-154, Vol. II.) the account of a ghostly experience of the author and his wife, which experience the writer of the paragraph, referring to this work in the notes to T. C. Croker's Banshee Stories, evidently considered was closely associated with the Banshee.

At the time of the incident, Lord Rossmore was Commander-in-Chief of the Forces in Ireland. He was a Scot by birth, but had come over to Ireland when very young, and had obtained the post of page to the Lord-Lieutenant. Fortune had favoured him at every turn. Not only had he been eminently successful in the vocation he finally selected, but he had been equally fortunate both with regard to love and money. The lady with whom he fell in love returned his affections, and, on their marriage, brought him a rich dowry. It was partly with her money that he purchased the estate of Mount Kennedy, and built on it one of the noblest mansions in Wicklow. Not very far from Mount Kennedy, and in the centre of what is termed the golden belt of Ireland, stood Dunran, the residence of the Barringtons; so that Lord Rossmore and the Barringtons were practically neighbours.

One afternoon at the drawing-room at Dublin Castle, during the Vice-royalty of Earl Hardwick, Lord Rossmore met Lady Barrington, and gave her a most pressing invitation to come to his house-party at Mount Kennedy the following day.

"My little farmer," said he, addressing her by her pet name, "when you go home, tell Sir Jonah that no business is to prevent him from bringing you down to dine with me to-morrow. I will have no ifs in the matter—so tell him that come he MUST."

Lady Barrington promised, and the following day saw her and Sir Jonah at Mount Kennedy. That night, at about twelve, they retired to rest, and towards two in the morning Sir Jonah was awakened by a sound of a very extraordinary nature. It occurred first at short intervals and resembled neither a voice nor an instrument, for it was softer than any voice, and wilder than any music, and seemed to float about in mid-air, now in one spot and now in another. To quote Sir Jonah's own language:

"I don't know wherefore, but my heart beat forcibly; the sound became still more plaintive, till it almost died in the air; when a sudden change, as if excited by a pang, changed its tone; it seemed descending. I felt every nerve tremble: it was not a natural sound, nor could I make out the point from whence it came. At length I awakened Lady Barrington, who heard it as well as myself. She suggested that it might be an Æolian harp; but to that instrument it bore no resemblance—it was altogether a different character of sound. My wife at first appeared less affected than I; but subsequently she was more so. We now went to a large window in our bedroom, which looked directly upon a small garden underneath. The sound seemed then, obviously, to ascend from a grass plot immediately below our window. It continued. Lady Barrington requested I would call up her maid, which I did, and she was evidently more affected than either of us. The sounds lasted for more than half an hour. At last a deep, heavy, throbbing sigh seemed to come from the spot, and was shortly succeeded by a sharp, low cry, and by the distinct exclamation, thrice repeated, of 'Rossmore!—Rossmore!—Rossmore!' I will not attempt to describe my own feelings," Sir Jonah goes on. "The maid fled in terror from the window, and it was with difficulty I prevailed on Lady Barrington to return to bed; in about a minute after the sound died gradually away until all was still."

Sir Jonah adds that Lady Barrington, who was not so superstitious as himself, made him promise he would not mention the incident to anyone next day, lest they should be the laughing stock of the place.

At about seven in the morning, Sir Jonah's servant, Lawler, rapped at the bedroom door and began, "Oh, Lord, sir!", in such agitated tones, that Sir Jonah at once cried out: "What's the matter?"

"Oh, sir," Lawler ejaculated, "Lord Rossmore's footman was running past my door in great haste, and told me in passing that my lord, after coming from the Castle, had gone to bed in perfect health (Lord Rossmore, though advanced in years, had always appeared to be singularly robust, and Sir Jonah had never once heard him complain he was unwell), but that about two-thirty this morning his own man, hearing a noise in his master's bed (he slept in the same room), went to him, and found him in the agonies of death; and before he could alarm the other servants, all was over."

Sir Jonah remarks that Lord Rossmore was actually dying at the moment Lady Barrington and he (Sir Jonah) heard his lordship's name pronounced; and he adds that he is totally unequal to the task of accounting for the sounds by any natural causes. The question that most concerns me is whether they were due to the Banshee or not, and as Lord Rossmore was not apparently of ancient Irish lineage, I am inclined to think the phenomena owed its origin to some other class of phantasm; perhaps to one that had been attached to Lord Rossmore's family in

Scotland. Moreover, I have never heard of the Banshee speaking as the invisible presence spoke on that occasion; the phenomena certainly seems to me to be much more Scottish than Irish.

CHAPTER VI
DUAL AND TRIPLE BANSHEE HAUNTINGS

It is a somewhat curious, and, perhaps, a not very well-known fact, that some families possess two Banshees, a friendly and an unfriendly one; whilst a few, though a few only, possess three—a friendly, an unfriendly, and a neutral one. A case of the two Banshees resulting in a dual Banshee haunting was told me quite recently by a man whom I met in Paris at Henriette's in Montparnasse. He was a Scot, a journalist, of the name of Menzies, and his story concerned an Irish friend of his, also a journalist, whom I will call O'Hara.

From what I could gather, these two men were of an absolutely opposite nature. O'Hara—warm-hearted, impulsive, and generous to a degree; Menzies—somewhat cold, careful with regard to money, and extremely cautious; and yet, apart from their vocation which was the apparent link between them, they possessed one characteristic in common—they both adored pretty women. The high brow and extreme feminist with her stolid features and intensely supercilious smile was a nightmare to them; they sought always something pleasing, and dainty, and free from academic conceits; and they found it in Paris—at Henriette's.

It so happened one day that, unable to get a table at Henriette's, the place being crowded, they wandered along the Boulevard Montparnasse, and turned into a new restaurant close to the Boulevard Raspail. This place, too, was very full, but there was one small table, at which sat alone a young girl, and, at O'Hara's suggestion, they at once made for it.

"You sly fellow," Menzies whispered to his friend, after they had been seated a few minutes, "I know why you were so anxious to come here."

"Well, wasn't I right," O'Hara, whose eyes had never once left the girl's face, responded. "She's the prettiest I've seen for many a day."

"Not bad!" Menzies answered, somewhat critically. "But I don't like her mouth, it's wolfish."

O'Hara, however, could see no fault in her; the longer he gazed at her, the deeper and deeper he fell in love; not that there was anything very unusual in that, because O'Hara was no sooner off with one flame than he was on with another; and he averaged at least two or three love cases a year. But to Menzies this latest affair was annoying; he knew that when O'Hara lost his heart he generally lost his head too, and could never talk or think on any topic but the eyes, hair, mouth and finger-nails—for, like most Irishmen, O'Hara had a passion for well-kept, well-formed hands—of his new divinity, and on this occasion he did want O'Hara to remain sane a little longer.

It was, then, for this reason chiefly, that Menzies did not get a little excited over the new discovery, too; for he was bound to admit that, in spite of the lupine expression about the mouth, there was some excuse this time for his friend's enthusiasm. The girl was pretty, an almost perfect blonde, with daintily shaped hands, and dressed as only a young Paris beauty can dress, who has money and leisure at her command.

Yes, there was excuse; and yet it was the height of folly. Girls mean expenditure in one way or another, and just now neither he nor O'Hara had anything to spend. While he was thinking, however, O'Hara was acting.

He offered the girl a cigarette, she smilingly rejected it; but the ice was broken, and the conversation begun. There is no need to go into any particulars as to what followed—it was what always did follow in a case of this description—blind infatuation that invariably ended with a startling abruptness; only in this instance the infatuation was blinder than ever, and the ending, though sudden, was not usual. O'Hara asked the girl to dinner with him that night. She accepted, and he took her out again the following evening. From that moment all reason left him, and he gave himself up to the maddest of mad passions.

Menzies saw little of him, but when they did by chance happen to meet it was always the same old tale—Gabrielle! Gabrielle Delacourt. Her star-like eyes, gorgeous hair, and so forth.

Then came a night when Menzies, tired of his own company, wandered off to Montmartre, and met a fellow-countryman of his, by name Douglas.

"I say, old fellow," the latter remarked, as they lolled over a little marble-topped table and watched the evolutions of a more than usually daring vaudeville artiste, "I say, how about that Irish pal of yours, 'O' something or other. I saw him here the other night with Marie Diblanc."

"Marie Diblanc!" Menzies articulated. "I have never heard of her."

"Not heard of Marie Diblanc!" Douglas exclaimed. "Why I thought every journalist in Paris knew of her, but perhaps she was before your time, for she's had a pretty long spell of prison—at least five or six years, which as you know is pretty stiff nowadays for a woman—and has only recently come out. She was quite a kiddie when they bagged her, but a kiddie with a mind as old as Brinvillier's in crime and vice—she robbed and all but murdered her own mother for a few louis, besides forging cheques and stealing wholesale from shops and hotels. They say she was in with all the worst crooks in Europe, and surpassed them all in subtlety and daring. When I saw her the other night her hair was dyed, and she was wearing the most saint-like expression; but I knew her all the same. She couldn't disguise her mouth or her hands, and it is those features that I notice in a woman more than anything else."

"Describe her to me," Menzies said.

"A brunette originally," Douglas replied, "but now a blonde—masses of very elaborately waved golden hair; peculiarly long eyes—rather too intensely blue and far apart for my liking—a well-moulded mouth, though the lips are far too thin, and give her away at once."

"That's the girl," Menzies exclaimed emphatically. "That's the girl he calls Gabrielle Delacourt. I was with him the day he first met her—over in Montparnasse."

Douglas nodded.

"That's right," he said. "That's the name he introduced her to me by. But, I'm quite positive she's Marie Diblanc; and I think you ought to give him the tip. If he's seen about with her he'll be suspected by the police. Besides, she is sure to commit some crime—for a girl with that kind of face and history never reforms, she goes on being right down bad to the bitter end—and get him implicated. Only, possibly, she will use him as her tool."

"I'll see him and warn him," Menzies said. "I'll call at his place to-night, though there's no knowing when he'll turn up, for he's the most erratic creature under the sun."

True to his word, Menzies, after a few more minutes' conversation, got up and retraced his steps to Montparnasse. O'Hara lived in the Rue Campagne Première, close to the famous "rabbit warren." His door, as not infrequently happened, was unlocked, but he was out. Menzies went in, and, entering the little room which served as a parlour, dining-room, and study combined, threw himself into an arm-chair and lit a cigarette. He did not bother to light up as it was a moonlight night, and the darkness suited his present mood. After a while, however, feeling a little chilly, he turned on the gas fire, and then, glancing at the clock over the mantel-shelf, perceived it was close on twelve.

At that instant there was a noise outside, and, thinking it was O'Hara, he called out, "Hulloa, Bob, is that you?"

As there was no response he called again, and this time there was a laugh—an ugly, malevolent kind of chuckle that made Menzies jump up at once and angrily demand who was there. No one replying, he went to the room door, and, opening it wide, saw a few yards from him a tall dark figure enveloped in what appeared to be a cloak and gown.

"Hulloa!" he cried. "Who are you, and what the — — do you want here?"

Whereupon the figure drew aside its covering and revealed a face that caused Menzies to utter an exclamation of terror and spring back. It was the face of an old woman with very high cheek-bones, tightly drawn shrivelled skin, and obliquely set pale eyes that gleamed banefully as they met Menzies' horrified stare. A disordered mass of matted yellow hair crowned her head and descended half-way to her shoulders, revealing, however, her ears, which stood out prominently from her head, huge and pointed, like those of an enormous wolf. A leadenish white glow seemed to emanate from within her and to intensify the general horror of her appearance.

Though Menzies had never believed in ghosts before, he felt certain now that he was looking at something which did not belong to this world. It was, he affirmed, so absolutely hellish that he would have uttered a prayer and bid it begone, had not his words died in his throat so that he could not articulate a sound. He then tried to raise a hand to cross himself, but this, also, he was unable to do; and the only thing he found he could do, was to stare at it in dumb, open-mouthed horror and wonder.

How long this state of affairs might have gone on it is impossible to say; but at the sound of heavy and unmistakably human footsteps, first in the lower part of the building, and then ascending the stone staircase leading to this flat, the old woman disappeared, apparently amalgamating with the somewhat artistic hangings on the wall behind her. Menzies was still rubbing his eyes and looking when O'Hara burst in upon him.

"Hulloa, Donald, is that you?" he began. "I've done it."

"Done what?" Menzies stuttered, his nerves all anyhow.

"Why, proposed to Gabrielle, of course," O'Hara went on excitedly, "and she's accepted me. She, the prettiest, sweetest, finest little colleen I've ever come across, has told me she will marry me. Ye gods, I shall go off my head with joy; go stark, staring mad, I tell you." And crossing the floor of the study he tumbled into the chair Menzies himself had just occupied.

"I say, old fellow, why don't you congratulate me?" he continued.

"I do congratulate you," Menzies observed, taking another seat. "Of course I congratulate you, but are you sure she is the sort of girl you will always care about or who will always care about you. You haven't known her very long, and most women cost a deuced lot of money, especially French ones. Don't take the irrevocable steps before contemplating them well first."

"I have," O'Hara retorted, "so it's no use sermonising. I have made up my mind to marry Gabrielle, and nothing on earth will deter me."

"Do you know her people, or anything about them?" Menzies ventured.

O'Hara laughed.

"No," he said, "but that doesn't bother me in the slightest. I shouldn't care whether her father was a navvy or a publican, or whether her mother took in washing and pinched a few odd shirts and socks now and again, only as it happens, they don't affect the question at all, because they are both dead. Gabrielle is an orphan—quite on her own—so I am perfectly safe as far as that goes. No pompous papa to consult, no cantankerous old mother-in-law to dread. Gabrielle was educated at a convent school, and, though you may laugh, knows next to nothing of the world. She's as innocent as a butterfly. We are to be married next month."

Finding that it was no earthly use to say any more on the subject, just then at all events, Menzies changed the conversation and referred to the incident of the old woman.

O'Hara at once became interested.

"Why," he said, "from your description she must have been one of the Banshees that is supposed to haunt our family, and which my mother always declared she saw shortly before my father's death. A hideous hag with a shock head of tow-coloured hair, who stood on the staircase laughing devilishly, and then, all at once, vanished. She is known as the bad Banshee to distinguish her from the good one, which is, so I have always been led to understand, very beautiful, but which never manifests itself, saving when anything especially dreadful is going to happen to an O'Hara."

Feeling very uneasy in his mind, Menzies now bid his friend good night, and went home.

After that days passed and Menzies saw nothing of O'Hara, until one evening, when he was thinking it must be about now that the marriage was to take place, O'Hara turned up at his flat, and proposed that they should go for a stroll in the direction of the fortifications near Montsouris. But O'Hara was not in his usual good spirits; he seemed very glum and depressed, and Menzies gathered that there had been occasional differences of opinion between his friend and Gabrielle, and that the affair was not running quite as smoothly as it might. Gabrielle had a great many admirers, one of them very rich, and O'Hara was obviously very much annoyed at the attentions they had been bestowing on his fiancée, and at the manner in which she had received them. But there was something else, too; something he could see in his friend's face and manner, but which O'Hara would not so much as hint at. Menzies was, of course, pleased, for there now seemed to be a glimmer of hope that these frictions would materialise into something stronger and more definite, and lead to a rupture that would be final.

He was so engrossed in speculations of this nature that he forgot all about the time or where they were, and was only brought back to earth by the whistle and shriek of a train, which made him at once realise they had left Montsouris and were several miles without the fortifications.

It was also getting very dusk, and, as he had to be up unusually early in the morning, he suggested to O'Hara they had better turn back. They were then close beside a clump of bushes and a very lofty pine tree that was bending to and fro in such a peculiar manner that Menzies' attention was at once directed to it.

"What's wrong with that tree?" he remarked, pointing at it with his stick.

"What's wrong with the tree?" O'Hara laughed. "Why, it's not the tree there's anything the matter with—the tree's all right, quite all right—it's you. What on earth are you staring at it for in that ridiculous fashion? Have you suddenly gone mad?"

Menzies made no reply, but went up to the tree and examined it. As he was doing so, a slight disturbance in the bushes made him glance around, and he saw, a few feet from him, the tall figure of a girl, clad in a kind of long flowing mantle, but with bare head and feet. The moonlight was on her face, and Menzies, hard and difficult though he was, as a rule, to please, realised it was lovely, far more lovely, so he declared afterwards, than any woman's face he had ever gazed upon. The eyes particularly impressed him, for, although in the darkness he could not tell their colour, he could see that they were of an extremely beautiful shape and setting, and seemed to be filled with a sorrow that was almost more than her heart could bear. Indeed, so poignant was this sorrow of hers, that Menzies, infected by it, too, could not keep back the tears from his own eyes; and, dour and unemotional as he was by nature, his whole being suddenly became literally steeped in sadness and pity.

The girl looked straight at him, but only for a few seconds; she then turned towards O'Hara, and seemed to concentrate her whole attention upon him. There was now, Menzies thought, a certain indistinctness and a something shadowy about her that he had not at first noticed, and he was thinking how he could test her to see if she were really a substance or merely an optical illusion, when O'Hara, who was getting tired at his long absence, called out, whereupon the girl at once vanished, uttering, as she melted away in the background, in the same inexplicable manner as the old woman had done, such an awful, harrowing, wailing shriek, that it seemed to fill the whole air, and to linger on for an eternity. Thoroughly terrified, Menzies, as soon as his scattered senses could collect themselves, fled from the spot, and didn't cease running till O'Hara's angry shout brought him to a standstill. To his astonishment O'Hara hadn't heard anything, and was only annoyed at his seemingly mad behaviour. In answer to his description of the girl, however, and the wailing, O'Hara at once declared it was the Banshee, and the one he had always been so particularly anxious to see.

"Unless you are having a joke at my expense," he said, "and you look too genuinely scared for that, you have actually seen her—a very beautiful girl, dressed after some old-time Irish custom, in a loose flowing green mantle—only of course you couldn't see the colour—with head and feet bare. But it's odd about that wail. The good Banshee in a family is always supposed to make it, but why didn't I hear her? Why should it only be you? You're Scotch, not Irish."

"For which I'm truly thankful," Menzies said with warmth. "I've lived without ever seeing or hearing a ghost or anything approaching one for thirty-eight years, and now I've seen and heard two, within the short space of three weeks, and all because of you, because you're Irish. No thanks. None of your Banshees for me. I'd rather, ten thousand times rather, be just an ordinary laddie from the Highlands, and dispense with your highly aristocratic and fastidious family ghost."

"Come, now," O'Hara said good-humouredly, "we won't quarrel about so unsubstantial a thing as the Banshee. Let's hurry up and have a bottle of cognac to make us think of something rather more cheerful."

Menzies often thought of those words, for it is not infrequently the most trifling words and actions that haunt our memory to the greatest extent in after days. The rest of the evening passed quite uneventfully, and, after they had "toasted" each other, the two friends separated for the night.

Two days later O'Hara's body lay in the Morque, whither it had been taken from the Seine. Though there were some doubts expressed as to the exact manner in which he had met his death, it was officially recorded "death from misadventure," and it was not till several years later Menzies learned the truth.

He was then in Mexico, in a little town not twenty miles from San Blas, on the

Western Coast, doing some newspaper work for a South American paper. A store-keeper and his wife were murdered; done to death in a singularly cruel manner, even for those parts, and one of the assassins was caught red-handed. The other, a woman, succeeded in escaping. As there had been so many murders lately in that neighbourhood, the townspeople declared they would make a very severe example of the culprit, and hang him, right away, on the scene of his diabolical outrage. Menzies, who had never witnessed anything of the kind before, and was, of course, anxious for copy, took good care to be present. He stood quite close to the handcuffed man, and caught every word of the confession he made to the local padre. He gave his name as André Fécamps, his age as twenty-five, and his nationality as French. He asserted that he was first induced to take to crime through falling in love with a notorious French criminal of the name of Marie Diblanc, who accepted him as her lover, conditionally on his joining the band of Apaches of which she was the recognised leader.

He did so, and forthwith plunged into every kind of wickedness imaginable. Among other crimes in which he was implicated he mentioned that of the murder of an Irishman of the name of O'Hara, who was supposed to have met with an accidental death from drowning in the Seine. What really happened, so the young desperado said, was this. M. O'Hara was madly in love with Marie Diblanc, who was posing to him as Gabrielle Delacourt, an innocent young girl from the country, when she was already very much married, and was being searched for high and low, at that very time, by certainly more than one desperate husband. Well, one day she persuaded M. O'Hara to take her to a dance given by some very wealthy friends of his.

He did so, and she contrived, unknown to him of course, to smuggle me in, and between us we walked off with something like ten thousand pounds of jewellery.

M. O'Hara came to suspect her—how I don't know, unless he overheard some stray conversation between her and some other member of our gang at one of the restaurants they used to dine at. Anyhow, she got to know of it, and at once resolved to have him put out of the way. It was arranged that she should bring him to a house in Montmartre, where several of us were in hiding, and that we should both kill and bury him there.

Well, he came, and, on perceiving that he had fallen into a trap, besought her, if his life must be forfeited—and, anyhow, now he knew she was a thief he wouldn't have it otherwise—to take it herself. This she eventually agreed to do, and, lying in her arms, he allowed her to press a poison-bag over his mouth, and so put him to death. His body was taken to the Seine that night in a fiacre and dropped in. Fécamps added that it was the only occasion upon which he had seen Marie Diblanc really moved, and he believed she was a trifle fond of the Irishman, that is to say, if she could be genuinely fond of anyone.

Menzies, who was of course deeply interested, extracted every particle of information he could out of the man, but nothing would make the latter admit a word as to what had become of Diblanc.

"If I go to hell," he said, "she is certain to go there, too; for bad as I am, I believe her to be infinitely worse; worse, a hundred times worse than any Apache man I have ever met. And yet, depraved and evil as she is, I love her, and shall never know a second's happiness till she joins me."

The man died; and Menzies, as he made a sketch of his swinging body, felt thoroughly satisfied at last that the ghost he had seen outside the fortifications of Monsouris was the good and beautiful Banshee, the Banshee that only manifested itself when some unusually dreadful fate was about to overtake an O'Hara.

CHAPTER VII
A SIMILAR CASE FROM SPAIN

Another case of dual Banshee haunting that occurs to me, took place in Spain, where so many of the oldest Irish families have settled, and was related to me by a distant connection of mine—an O'Donnell. He well remembered, he said, many years ago, when he was a boy, his father, who was an officer in the Carlist Army, telling him of an adventure that happened to him during the first outbreak of the Civil War. His father and another young man, Dick O'Flanagan, were subalterns in a cavalry regiment that took a prominent part in a desperate engagement with the Queen's Army. The Carlists were being driven back, when, as a last desperate resource, their bare handful of cavalry charged and immediately turned the fortunes of the day. In the heat of the affray, however, Ralph O'Donnell and Dick O'Flanagan, carried away by their enthusiasm, got separated from the rest of the corps, and were, consequently, overpowered by sheer numbers and taken prisoners.

In those days much brutality was shown on either side, and our two heroes, beaten, and bruised, and starving, were dragged along in a half-fainting condition, amid the taunts and gibings of their captors, till they were finally lodged in the filthy dungeon of an old mountain castle, where they were informed they would be kept till the hour appointed for their execution. The moment they were alone, they made the most strenuous efforts to unloosen the thongs of tough cowhide with which their hands and feet were so cruelly bound together, and, after many frantic endeavours, they at last succeeded. O'Flanagan was the first to get free, and as soon as his numbed limbs allowed him to do so, he crawled to the side of his friend and liberated him, too. They then examined the room as best they could in the dark, and decided their only hope of escape lay in the chimney, which, luckily for them, was one of those old-fashioned structures, wide enough to admit the passage of a full-grown person. Ralph began the ascent first, and, after several fruitless efforts, during which he bumped and bruised himself and made such a noise that O'Flanagan feared he would be heard by the guard outside, he eventually managed to obtain a foothold and make sufficient progress for O'Flanagan to follow in his wake.

In everything they did that night luck favoured them. On emerging from the chimney on to the roof of the castle, they were rejoiced to find a tree growing so near to one of the walls that they had little difficulty in gripping hold of one of its branches and so descending in safety to the ground. The guards apparently were asleep, at least none were to be seen anywhere, and so, feeling their way cautiously in and out a thick growth of trees and bushes, they soon got altogether clear of the premises, and found themselves once again free, but in a part of the country with which they were totally unacquainted. Two hours tramping along a tortuous, hilly high road, or to give it a more appropriate name, track, for it was nothing more, at last brought them to a wayside inn where, in spite of the advanced hour—for it was between one and two o'clock in the morning—they determined to risk inquiry for a night's shelter. I say "risk" because there was a strong spirit of partisanship abroad, and it was quite as likely as not that the inn people were adherents of the Queen.

Ralph knocked repeatedly, and the door was at length opened by a young girl who, holding a candlestick in one hand, sleepily rubbed her eyes with the other and, in rather petulant tones, asked what the gentlemen meant by coming to the house at such an unearthly hour and waking everyone up. Ralph and O'Flanagan were so struck by her appearance that for some seconds they could only stand gaping at her, deprived of all power of speech. Such a vision of loveliness neither of them had seen for many a long day, and both were more than ordinarily susceptible where the fair sex was concerned. Dark, like most of the girls are in Spain, she was not swarthy, but had, on the other hand, a most singularly fair complexion, devoid of that tendency to hairiness which is apparent in so many of the women of that country. Her features were, perhaps, a trifle too bold, but in strict proportion, and her eyes a wee bit hard, though the shape and colour of them—by candlelight an almost purplish grey—were singularly beautiful. She had very white teeth, too, though there was a something about her mouth, in the setting of the lips when they were closed for instance, and in the general expression, that puzzled Ralph, and which was destined to return to his mind many times afterwards.

Ralph noticed, too, that her hands were not those of a peasant class, of a class that has to do much rough and hard work, but that they were white and well-kept, the fingers tapering and the nails long and almond shaped. She wore several rings and bracelets, and seemed altogether different from the type of girl one would have expected to find in such a very unpretentious kind of building, situated, too, in such a very remote spot.

Ralph was not quite as impulsive as his friend, and although, as I have said, very susceptible, was not so far led away by his feelings as to be altogether incapable of observation.

His first impressions of the girl were that, although she was extraordinarily pretty, there was something—apart even from her mouth—that he could not fathom, and which caused him a vague uneasiness; he noticed it particularly when her glance wandered to their travel-stained uniforms, and momentarily alighted on O'Flanagan's solitary ring, which contained a ruby and was a kind of family mascot, akin to the famous cathach of Count Daniel O'Donnell of Tirconnell; and she muttered something which Ralph fancied had reference to the word "Carlists," and then, as if conscious he was watching her, she raised her eyes quickly and, in tones of sleepy indifference this time, asked what the gentlemen wanted. Ralph immediately replied that they required a bed with breakfast, not too early, and, perhaps, later on—luncheon. He added that if the inn was full they wouldn't in the least mind sleeping in a barn or stable.

"All we want," he said, "is to lie down somewhere with a roof over our heads, for we are terribly tired."

At the mention of a stable the girl smiled, saying she could offer them something rather better than that; and, bidding both follow her upstairs, with as little noise as possible, she conducted them to a large room with a very low ceiling, and, having deposited the candlestick on a chest of drawers, she wished them good night and noiselessly withdrew.

"Rather better than our late quarters in the prison," Ralph exclaimed, taking a survey of the apartment, "but a wee bit gloomy."

"Nonsense!" O'Flanagan retorted. "The only gloomy things here are your own thoughts. I want to stay here always, for I never saw a prettier girl or a cosier-looking bed."

He began to undress as he spoke, and in a few minutes both young men were stretched out at full length fast asleep.

About two hours later Ralph awoke with a violent start to hear distinct sounds of footsteps tiptoeing their way softly along the passage outside towards their room door. In an instant all his faculties were on the alert, and he sat up in bed and listened. Then something stirred in the corner by the window, and, glancing in that direction, he saw to his astonishment the figure of a tall slim girl, in a long, loose, flowing gown of some dark material, with a very pale face, beautifully chiselled, though by no means strictly classical features, and masses of shining golden hair that fell in rippling confusion on to her neck and shoulders. The idea that she was the Banshee instantly occurred to him. From his father's description of her, for his father had often spoken to him about her, she and the beautiful woman, whom he was now looking at, were certainly very much alike; besides, as the Banshee, when his father saw her, was crying, and this woman was crying—crying most bitterly, her whole body swaying to and fro as if racked with the most poignant sorrow—he could not help thinking that the identity between them was established, and that they were, in fact, one and the same person.

As he was still gazing at her with the most profound pity and admiration, his attention was suddenly directed, by an odd scratching sound, to the window, where he saw, pressed against the glass, and looking straight in at him, a face which in every detail presented the most startling contrast to that upon which his eyes had, but a second ago, been feasting. It was so evil that he felt sure it could only emanate from the lowest Inferno, and it leered at him with such appalling malignancy that, brave man as he had proved himself on the field of battle, he now completely lost his nerve, and would have called out, had not both figures suddenly vanished, their disappearance being immediately followed by the most agonising, heart-rending screams, intermingled with loud laughter and diabolical chuckling, which, for the moment, completely paralysed him. The screams continued for some seconds, during which time every atom of blood in Ralph's veins seemed to freeze, and then there was silence—deep and sepulchral silence. Afraid to be any longer in the dark, Ralph jumped out of bed and lit the candle, and, as he did so, he distinctly heard footsteps move hurriedly away from the door and go stealthily tiptoeing down the passage.

As may be imagined, he did not sleep again for some time, not, indeed, until daylight, when he gradually fell into a doze, from which he was eventually aroused by loud thumps on the door, and the voice of the pretty inn maiden announcing that it was time to get up.

After breakfast he narrated his experience in the night to O'Flanagan, who, somewhat to his astonishment, did not laugh, but exclaimed quite seriously:

"Why, you have seen our Banshee. At least, the girl in green is our Banshee. I saw her before the death of a cousin of mine, and she appeared to my mother the night before my father died. I don't know what the other apparition could have been, unless it was what my father used to term the 'hateful Banshee,' which he said was only supposed to appear before some very dreadful catastrophe, worse even than death, if anything could be worse."

"You haven't the monopoly of Banshees," Ralph laughed. "We have one too, and I am positive the woman I saw—the beautiful woman I mean—was the O'Donnell Banshee. I would have you know that the Limerick O'Donnells, with whom I am connected, are quite as old a family as the O'Flanagans; they are, indeed, directly descended from Niall of the Nine Hostages."

"So are we," O'Flanagan answered hotly, then he burst out laughing. "Well, well," he said, "fancy quarrelling about anything as immaterial as a Banshee. But, anyhow, if they were Banshees that you saw last night, they're a bit out in their calculations. They should have come before that skirmish, not after it; unless it's the death of some relative of one of us they're prophesying. I hope it's not my sister."

"I don't imagine it has anything to do with you," Ralph replied. "They were both looking at me."

He was about to say something further, when O'Flanagan, seeing the young girl come into the room to clear away the breakfast things, at once began talking to her; and as it was only too evident that he wanted the field to himself, for he was obviously head over ears in love, Ralph got up and announced his intention of taking a walk round the premises.

"Don't go in the wood, Señor, whatever you do," the girl observed, "for it is infested with brigands. They do not interfere with us because we were once good to one of their sick folk—and the Spaniard, brigand though he may be, never forgets a kindness—but they attack strangers, and you will be well advised to keep to the high road."

"Which is the nearest town?" Ralph demanded.

"Trijello," the girl answered, the same curious expression creeping into her eyes that had puzzled Ralph so much before, and which he found impossible to analyse. "It is about eight miles from here. Don Hervado, the Governor, is a Carlist, and was entertaining some Carlist soldiers there yesterday."

"Good!" Ralph exclaimed. "I will walk there. Will you come with me, Dick, or will you wait here till I return. I don't suppose I shall be back much before the evening."

"Oh, don't hurry," O'Flanagan laughed, eyeing the girl rapturously, "I am perfectly happy here, and want a rest badly. Don't, whatever you do, let on to anyone connected with headquarters where we are. Let them go on imagining, for a while, we are dead."

"The Señors have been in a battle, yes?" the girl interrupted, shyly.

"A battle," O'Flanagan laughed, "not half one. Why, we were taken prisoners and only escaped hanging through my unparalleled wits and perseverance. However, I don't in the least bemoan the perils and hardships we have undergone, for, had events turned out otherwise, we should never have had the joy of seeing you, Señora," and catching hold of her hand, before she could prevent him, he pressed it fervently to his lips, smothering it with kisses.

Thinking it was high time to be off, Ralph now took his departure. A couple of hours' walking brought him to Trijello, where, but for a lucky incident, he might have found himself landed in a quandary. As he was entering the outskirts of the town he met an old peasant, staggering under a sack of onions, and no sooner did the latter catch sight of his uniform than he at once called out:

"Señor, if you value your liberty, you won't enter Trijello in that costume. The Governor is the sworn enemy of all Carlists, and has given strict orders that, anyone with leanings towards that party shall be put under arrest at once."

"Are you sure?" Ralph exclaimed. "Why, I was told it was just the other way about, and that he was a strong adherent of our cause."

"Whoever told you that, lied," the old man responded, "for he had a nephew of mine shot only yesterday morning for saying in public he hoped that wretched weakling of a woman would soon be put off the throne and we should have someone who was fit to govern—meaning Don Carlos—in her place. Take my advice, Señor, and either change those clothes at once or give Trijello as wide a berth as possible."

Ralph then asked him if there was any place near at hand where he could purchase a civilian suit, and, on being informed that there was a Jew's shop within a few minutes' walk, he thanked the old man most cordially for giving him so friendly a warning, and at once proceeded there.

To cut a long story short he bought the clothes and, thus disguised, went on into the town, and, with the object of picking up any information he could with regard to the enemy's forces, he dined at the principal hotel, and listened attentively to the conversation that was taking place all around him. Later on in the day some Christino soldiers arrived, officers on the staff of one of the Royalist generals, and Ralph decided to remain in the hotel for the night and see if he could get hold of some really definite news that might be of value to his own headquarters. Learning that someone would be leaving the hotel shortly and passing by the inn where O'Flanagan was staying, he gave them a note to give to his friend, stating that he could not be back till the following day, perhaps about noon. He then took up his seat before the parlour fire, apparently absorbed in reading the latest bulletin from Madrid, but in reality keeping his ears well open for any conversation that might be worth transcribing in his pocket-book. Nor was he disappointed, for the Christino soldiers waxed very talkative over some of mine host's best port, and disclosed many secrets concerning the movements of the Queen's forces, that would have most certainly entailed a court martial, had it but come to the notice of their general.

That night, though the room he was given was quite bright and cheerful, and very different from the one he had occupied the night before, his mind was so full of grim apprehension that he found it quite impossible to sleep. He kept thinking of the vision he had seen—that lovely, fairy face of the girl with the golden hair, her adorable eyes, her heavenly, albeit very human mouth; she was so perfect, so angelic, so full of delicious sympathy and pity; so unlike any earthly woman he had ever met; and then that other face—those intensely evil, pale green eyes, that sinister mocking mouth, that dreadfully disordered mass of matted, tow-coloured hair. It was too hellish—too inconceivably foul and baneful to dare think about, and seized with a fit of shuddering, he thrust his head under the bedclothes, lest he should see it again appearing before him. What, he wondered, did they portend? Not some horrible happening to Dick. He had always understood that the one who neither sees nor hears the Banshee during its manifestations is the one that is doomed to die. And yet Dick was assuredly as safe in that inn as he was here—here, surrounded on all sides by his enemies. Once or twice he fancied he heard his name called, and so realistic was it, that, forgetful of his dread of seeing something satanic in the room, he at last sat up in bed and listened. All was still, however; there were no sounds at all; none whatever, saving the gentle whispering of the wind, as it swept softly past the window, and the far-away hooting of a night bird. Then he lay down again, and once more there seemed to come to him from somewhere very close at hand a voice that articulated very clearly and plaintively his name—Ralph, Ralph, Ralph!—three times in quick succession, and then ceased. Nor did he hear it again.

Tired and unrested, he got up early and, paying his bill, set off with long, rapid strides in the direction of the wayside inn. There was an air of delightful peace and tranquillity about the place when he arrived. All the sunbeams seemed to have congregated in just that one spot, and to have converted the walls and window-panes of the little old-fashioned building into sheets of burnished gold. Birds twittered merrily on the tree-tops and under the eaves of the roof, and the most delicious smell of honeysuckle and roses permeated the whole atmosphere.

Ralph was enchanted, and all his grim forebodings of the night before were instantly dissipated. The abode was truly named "The Travellers' Rest"; it might even have been styled "The Travellers' Paradise," for all seemed so calm and serene—so truly heavenly. He rapped at the door, and, after some moments, rapped again. He then heard footsteps, which somehow seemed strangely familiar, cautiously come along the stone passage and pause at the other side of the door, as if their owner were in doubt whether to open it or not.

Again he rapped, and this time the door was opened, and the young girl appeared. She looked rather pale, but was very much sprucer and smarter than she had been when Ralph last saw her. She wore a very bewitching kind of gipsy frock of red velvet—the skirt very short and the bodice adorned with masses of shining silver coins, whilst her feet were clad in very smart, dainty shoes, also red, with big silver buckles.

"Your friend's gone," she said. "He seemed very upset at your not turning up last night, and went away directly after breakfast."

"But didn't he get my note?" Ralph exclaimed, "and didn't he leave any message?"

"No, Señor," the girl replied. "No note came for him, but he said he would try and call in here again to-morrow morning, to see if you had arrived."

"And he didn't say where he had gone?"

"No."

Ralph eyed her quizzically. She certainly was wonderfully pretty, and, marvellous to relate, did not smell of garlic. Yes, he would stay, and try and come under the fascination of her beauty as Dick had done. And yet, why had Dick gone off in such a hurry? What had this starry-eyed creature done to offend him? Ralph knew O'Flanagan was at times apt to be over-impulsive and hasty in his love-makings. Had he got on a bit too rapidly? Spanish girls are very easily upset, and perhaps this one had a lover in the background. Perhaps she was married. That seemed to him the most feasible explanation for Dick's absence. To be offended at his not turning up last night was all nonsense. Ralph knew his friend far too well for that. Anyhow, he decided to stay, and the girl offered him the room he and Dick had previously occupied. Only, she explained, he must not go in it till later on in the day, as it was going to be cleaned.

After luncheon, which he sat down to alone, as the girl, despite his pressing invitation, refused to partake of the meal with him, on the plea that she had many things to attend to, he went a little way up the hillside at the back of the premises, and enjoyed a quiet siesta under the shadow of the trees. Indeed, he slept so long that the twilight had well set in before he awoke and once again made tracks for the inn.

This time he entered by a doorway in the rear of the house, and, in a small paved courtyard, saw the girl, habited in a rather more workaday attire, but with her hair still very coquettishly decorated with ribbons, sharpening a long glistening knife on a big grinding stone, which she was turning round and round with the skill of a past mistress of the art.

"Hulloa!" he exclaimed. "What are you up to? Not sharpening that blade to stick me with, I hope."

"The Señor has heard of pigs," the girl replied, showing her beautiful teeth in a smile, almost amounting to a grin. "Well, I'm going to kill one to-night."

"Good heavens!" Ralph ejaculated, glancing incredulously at the white, rounded arms and the long, slim, tapering fingers. "You kill a pig! Do you do all the work of this house? Is there no one else here to help you?"

"Oh, yes, Señor," the girl laughed. "There is Isabella, an old woman who comes here every day to do all the hard rough work, and my aunt, but there are certain jobs they can't do because their eyesight is not very good, and their hands lack the skill. The gentleman looks shocked, but is there anything so very dreadful in killing a pig? One slash and it is quickly done—very quickly. We have to live somehow, and, after all, the Señor is a soldier—he follows the vocation of killing!"

"Oh, yes, it is all very well for big, rough men. One somehow associates them with deeds of violence and bloodshed. But with beautiful, dainty girls like you it is different. You should shudder at the very thought of blood, and be all pity and compassion."

"But not for pigs," the girl laughed, "nor for Señors. Now please go in and sit in the parlour, or my aunt will hear me talking to you and accuse me of wasting my time."

Ralph reluctantly obeyed, and drawing his chair close up to the parlour fire—for the summer evenings in Spain are often very chilly—was soon deeply absorbed in plans and speculations as to the future. After supper, when the young girl came into the room to clear the table, Ralph noticed that she was once again wearing the gay apparel she had worn earlier in the day; and all in red, even to the ribbons in her hair, she seemed to be dressed more coquettishly than ever. She was also inclined to be more communicative, and in response to Ralph's invitation to partake of a glass of wine with him, she fetched an armchair and came and planted it close beside him.

Pretty as he had thought her before, she now appeared to him to be indescribably lovely, and the longer he stared at her, stared into the depths of her large, beautifully shaped purplish grey eyes, the more and more hopelessly enslaved did he become, till, in the end, he realised she had him completely at her mercy, and that he was most madly and desperately in love with her.

They drank together, and so absorbed was he in gazing at her eyes—indeed he never ceased gazing at them—that he did not observe what he was drinking or how many times she filled up his glass. If she had given him a poisoned goblet, it would have been all the same, he would have drained it off and kissed her hands and feet with his dying breath.

"Now, Señor," she said at length, after he had held her hand to his lips and literally smothered it in kisses, "now, Señor, it is time for you to go to bed. We do not keep late hours here, and to-morrow, Señor, if he is still in the same state of mind, will have plenty of time for repeating to me his sentiments."

"To-morrow," Ralph stuttered. "To-morrow, that is a tremendous way off, and isn't it to-morrow that that fellow O'Flanagan is coming?"

The girl laughed. "Yes," she said saucily, "there will be two of you to-morrow, the one as bad as the other, and I did think, Señor, you were the steadier of the two. Well, well, you are both soldiers, and soldiers were ever gay dogs; but you must be careful, Señor, you and your friend do not quarrel, for, as you know, more than one friendship has been terminated through the witching glance of a lady's eyes, and you both seem to like looking into mine."

"What!" Ralph stuttered angrily. "Did that fellow Dick look at you? Did he dare to look at you? Damn — —" but before he could utter another syllable, the girl put her soft little hand over his mouth and pushed him gently to the door.

Alternately making wild love to her and passionately denouncing Dick, Ralph then allowed himself to be got upstairs to his room by pushes and coaxings, and, as he made a last frantic effort to kiss and fondle her, the door slammed in his face and he found himself—alone.

For some moments he stood tugging and twisting at the door handle, and then, finding that his efforts had no effect, he was staggering off to the bed with the intention of getting into it just as he was, when he caught his foot on something and fell with a crash to the floor, striking his face smartly on the edge of a chair. For a moment or so he was partially stunned, but, the flow of blood from his nose relieving him, he gradually came to his senses, all trace of his drunkenness having completely vanished. The first thing he did then was to look at the carpet which, by a stroke of luck, was crimson, a most pronounced, virulent crimson, exactly the colour of his blood. The spot where he had fallen was close to the bed, and, as his eyes wandered along the carpet by the side of the bed, he fancied he saw another damp patch. He at once fetched the candle and had a closer look.

Yes, there was a great splash of moisture on the floor, near the head of the bed, just about in a line with the pillow. He applied his finger to the patch and then held it to the light—it was wet with blood.

Filled with a sickening sense of apprehension, Ralph now proceeded to make a careful examination of the room, and, lifting the lid of a huge oak chest that stood in one corner, he was horrified to perceive the naked body of a man lying at the bottom of it, all huddled up.

Gently raising the body and bending down to examine it, Ralph received a second shock. The face that looked up at him with such utter lack of expression in its big, bulging, glassy eyes was that of the once gay and humorous Dick O'Flanagan.

The manner of his death was only too obvious. His throat had been cut, not cleanly as a man would have done it, but with repeated hacks and slashes, that pointed all too clearly to a woman's handiwork.

This then explained it all, explained the curious something in the girl's eyes and mouth he had noticed when he first saw her; explained, too, the stealthy, tiptoeing footsteps in the passage that night, the reason for the appearance of the Banshees, the eagerness with which the girl had plied him with wine, her red dress—and—the red carpet.

But why had she done it—for mere sordid robbery, or because they were Carlists. Then recollecting the look she had fixed on the ruby in Dick's ring, the answer seemed clear. It was, of course, robbery. Snake-like, she used those beautiful eyes of hers to fascinate her victims—to lull them into a false sense of security; and then, when they had wholly succumbed to love and wine, of which she gave them their fill, she butchered them.

Murders in Spanish inns were by no means uncommon about that time, and even at a much later date, and had this murder been committed by some old and ugly and cross-grained "host," Ralph would not have been surprised, but for this girl to have done it—this girl so young and enchanting, why it was almost inconceivable, and he would not have believed it, had not the grim proofs of it lain so close at hand. What was he to do? Of course, now that he was sober and in the full possession of his faculties, it was ridiculous for him to be afraid of a girl, even though she were armed; but supposing she had confederates, and it was scarcely likely she would be alone in the house.

No, he must try and escape; but how! He examined the window, it was heavily barred; he tried the door, it was locked on the outside; he looked up the chimney, it was far too narrow to admit the passage of anyone even half his size.

He was done, and the only thing he could do was to wait. To wait till the girl tiptoed into the room to kill, and then—he couldn't bear the idea of fighting with her, even though she had so cruelly murdered poor Dick—make his escape.

With this end in view he blew out the candle, and, lying on the bed, pretended to be fast asleep.

In about an hour's time he heard steps, soft, cautious footsteps, ascend the staircase and come stealing surreptitiously towards his door. Then they paused, and he instinctively knew she was listening. He breathed heavily, just as a man would do who had drunk not wisely but too well, and had consequently fallen into a deep sleep. Presently, there was a slight movement of the door handle.

He continued breathing, and the movement was repeated. Still more stentorian breaths, and the handle this time was completely turned. Very gently he crept off the bed to the door, and, as it slowly opened and a figure in red, looking terribly ghostly and sinister, slipped in, so he suddenly shot past and made a bolt for the passage. There was a wild shriek, something whizzed past his head and fell with a loud clatter on the floor, and all the doors in the house downstairs seemed to open simultaneously. Reaching the head of the stairs in a few bounds, he was down them in a trice. A hideous old hag rushed at him with a hatchet, whilst another aged creature, whose sex he could not determine, aimed a wild blow at him with some other instrument, but Ralph avoided them both, and, reaching the front door, which providentially for him was merely locked, not bolted, he was speedily out of the house and into the broad highway.

The screams of the women producing answering echoes from the wood in the hoarser shouts of men, Ralph took to his heels, nor did he stop running until he was well on his way to Trijello.

He did not, however, go to the latter town, fearing that the inn people might follow him there and get him arrested as a Carlist; instead, he struck off the high road along a side path, and, luckily for him, about noon fell in with an advanced guard of the Carlist Army.

His troubles then, for a time at least, ceased; but to his lasting regret he was never able to avenge Dick's death; for when the war was at last over and he had succeeded in persuading the local authorities to take the matter in hand, the inn was found to be empty and deserted. Nor was the pretty murderess ever seen or heard of again in that neighbourhood.

CHAPTER VIII

THE BANSHEE ON THE BATTLE-FIELD

Although the Banshee haunting referred to in my last chapter occurred during a war, the manifestations did not take place on the battle-field; nor were they actually due to the fighting. At the same time it cannot be denied that they were the outcome of it, for had our two lieutenants not been fighting desperately in a skirmish and got separated from the main body of the Army, in all probability they never would have visited the wayside inn, and the Banshee manifestations there would never have occurred.

There are, however, many instances on record of Banshee manifestations occurring on the battle-field, either immediately before or after, or even whilst the fighting was actually taking place. Mr McAnnaly, in his "Irish Wonders," p. 117, says:

> "Before the Battle of the Boyne, Banshees were heard singing in the air over the Irish camp, the truth of the prophecy being verified by the death roll of the next morning."

Now several of my own immediate ancestors took part in the Battle of the Boyne[10], and according to a family tradition one of them both saw and heard the Banshee. He was sitting in the camp, the night prior to the fighting, conversing with several other officers, including his brother Daniel, when, feeling an icy wind coming from behind and blowing down his back, he turned round to look for his cloak which he had discarded a short time before, owing to the heat from a fire close beside them. The cloak was not there, and, as he turned round still further to look for it, he perceived to his astonishment the figure of a woman, swathed from head to foot in a mantle of some dark flowing material, standing a few feet behind him. Wondering who on earth she could be, but supposing she must be a relative or friend of one of the officers, for her mantle looked costly, and her hair—of a marvellous golden hue—though hanging loose on her shoulders, was evidently well cared for, he continued to gaze at her with curiosity. Then he gradually perceived that she was shaking—shaking all over, with what he at first imagined must be laughter; but from the constant clenching of her hands and heaving of her bosom, he finally realised that she was weeping, and he was further assured on this point, when a sudden gust of wind, blowing back her mantle, he caught a full <u>view of her face.</u>

[10] It may be recorded here as a matter of interest that my ancestress, Helena Sarsfield, was a daughter of James Sarsfield, great-uncle of Patrick Sarsfield, Earl of Lucan and the defender of Limerick against the English.

Its beauty electrified him. Her cheeks were as white as marble, but her features were perfect, and her eyes the most lovely he had ever seen. He was about to address her, to inquire if he could be of any service to her, when, someone calling out and asking him what on earth he was doing, she at once began to melt away, and, amalgamating with the soft background of grey mist that was creeping towards them from the river, finally disappeared.

He thought of her, however, some hours later, when they were all lying down, endeavouring to snatch a few hours' sleep, and presently fancied he saw, in dim, shadowy outline, her fair face and figure, her big, sorrowful eyes, gazing pitifully first at one and then at another of his companions, but particularly at one, a mere boy, who was lying wrapped in his military cloak, close beside the smouldering embers of the fire. He fancied that she approached this youths and, bending over him, stroked his short, curly hair with her delicate fingers.

Thinking that possibly he might be asleep and dreaming, he rubbed his eyes vigorously, but the outlines were still there, momentarily becoming stronger and stronger, more and more distinct, until he realised with a great thrill that she actually was there, just as certainly as she had been when he had first seen her.

He was so intent watching her and wishing she would leave the youth and come to him, that he did not notice that one of his comrades had seen her, too, until the latter, who had raised himself into a half-sitting posture, spoke; then, just as before, the figure of the girl melted away, and seemed to become absorbed in the dark and shadowy background.

A moment later, he heard, just over his head, a loud moaning and wailing that lasted for several seconds and then died away in one long, protracted sob that suggested mental anguish of an indescribably forlorn and hopeless nature.

The deaths of most of his companions of the night, including that of the curly haired boy, occurred on the following day.

But the Banshee, although of course appearing to soldiers of Irish birth only, does not confine its attentions to those who are fighting on their native soil; it has been stated that she frequently manifested herself to Irishmen engaged on active service abroad during the Napoleonic Wars, and also to those serving in America during the Civil War.

With regard to the Banshee demonstrations in connection with the Napoleonic campaigns, I have not been able to acquire any written record; but as the result of numerous letters sent out by me broadcast in quest of information, I was asked by several people to call either at their houses or clubs, and, gladly accepting their invitations, I learned from them the incidents which, with their permission, I am now about to relate.

Miss O'Higgins, an aged lady, residing, prior to the late war, close to Fifth Avenue, New York, and visiting, when I met her, a friend in the Rue Campagne Première, Paris, told me that she well remembered her grandfather telling her when she was a child that he heard the Banshee at Talavera, a day or two prior to the great battle. He was serving with the Spanish Army, having married the daughter of a Spanish officer, and had no idea at the time that there were any men of Irish extraction in his corps. Bivouacking with about a hundred other soldiers in a valley, and happening to awake in the night with an ungovernable thirst, he made his way down to the banks of the river that flowed near by, drank his fill, and was in the act of returning, when he was startled to hear a most agonising scream, quickly followed by another, and then another, all proceeding apparently from the camp, whither he was wending his steps. Wondering what on earth could have happened, and inclining to the belief that it must be in some way connected with one of those women thieves who prowled about everywhere at night, robbing and murdering, with equal impunity, wherever they saw a chance, he quickened his pace, only to find, on his arrival at the camp, no sign whatever of the presence of any woman, although the screaming was going on as vigorously as ever. The sounds seemed to come first from one part of the camp, and then from another, but to be always overhead, as if uttered by invisible beings, hovering at a height of some six or seven feet, or, perhaps, more, above the ground, and although Lieutenant O'Higgins had at first attributed these sounds to one person only, on listening attentively he fancied he could detect several different voices— all women's—and he eventually came to the conclusion that at least three or four phantasms must have been present. As he stood there listening, not knowing what else to do, the wailing and sobbing seemed to grow more and more harrowing, until it affected him so much that, hardened as he had become to all kinds of misery and violence, he, too, felt like weeping, out of sheer sympathy. However, this state of affairs did not last long, for at the sound of a musket shot (that of a sentry, as Lieutenant O'Higgins afterwards ascertained, giving a false alarm in some distant part of the camp) the wailing and sobbing abruptly and completely ceased, and was never, the Lieutenant declared, heard by him again.

On mentioning the matter to one of his brother officers in the morning, the latter, no little interested and surprised, at once said: "You have undoubtedly heard the Banshee. Poor D— —, who fell at Corunna, often used to tell me about it, and, you may depend upon it, there are some Irishmen in camp now, and it was their funeral dirge that you listened to."

What he said proved to be quite correct, for, on inquiring, Lieutenant O'Higgins discovered three of the soldiers who had been sleeping around him that evening had Irish names, and were, unquestionably, of ancient Irish origin; and all of them perished on the bloody field of Talavera, twenty-four hours later.

A story relating to an O'Farrell, who was with the Spanish in the same war, was also told me by Miss O'Higgins; but whether this O'Farrell was the famous general of that name or not I do not know. The story ran as follows:[11]

It was the day prior to the fall of Badajoz, and O'Farrell, who was in Badajoz at the time, a prisoner of the French, was invited to partake of supper with some Spanish-Irish friends of his of the name of McMahon. The French, it may be observed, were, as a rule, rather more lenient to their Irish prisoners than to their English, and O'Farrell was allowed to ramble about Badajoz in perfect freedom, a mere pledge being extracted from him that he wouldn't stroll outside the bound-

[11] Neither of her stories have appeared in print before.

aries of the town without special permission. On the night in question O'Farrell left his quarters in high spirits. He liked the McMahons, especially the youngest daughter Katherine, with whom he was very much in love. He deemed his case hopeless, however, as Mr McMahon, who was poor, had often said none of his daughters should marry, unless it were someone who was wealthy enough to ensure them being well provided for, should they be left a widow; and as O'Farrell had nothing but his pay, which was meagre enough in all conscience, he saw no prospect of his ever being able to propose to the object of his affections. Had he been strong-minded enough, he told himself, he would have at once said good-bye to Katherine, and never have allowed himself to see or even think of her again; but, poor weakling that he was, he could not bear the idea of taking a final peep into her eyes—the eyes that he had idealised into his heaven and everything that made life worth living for—and so he kept accepting invitations to their house and throwing himself across her path, whenever the slightest opportunity presented itself.

And now he found himself once more speeding to meet her, telling himself repeatedly that it should be the last time, but at the same time making up his mind that it should be nothing of the sort. He arrived at the house far too early, of course—he always did—and was shown into a room to wait there till the family had finished their evening toilets. Large glass doors opened out of the room on to a veranda, and O'Farrell, stepping out on to the latter, leaned over the iron railings, and gazed into the semi-courtyard, semi-garden below, in the centre of which was a fountain surmounted by the marble statue of a very beautiful maiden, that his instinct told him was an exact image of his beloved Katherine. He was gazing at it, revelling in the delightful anticipation of meeting the flesh and blood counterpart of it in a very short time, when sounds of music, of someone playing a very, very sad and plaintive air on the harp, came to him through the open doorway. Much surprised, for none of the family as far as he knew were harpists, nor had he, indeed, ever seen a harp in the house, he turned round; but, to add to his astonishment, no one was there. The room was apparently just as empty as when he had been ushered into it, and yet the music unquestionably emanated from it. Considerably mystified, for every now and then there was a peculiar far-offness in the sounds which he could liken to nothing he had ever heard before, he remained on the veranda, prevented by a strange feeling of awe, and something very akin to dread, from venturing into the room.

He was thus occupied, half standing and half leaning against the framework of the glass door, when the harping abruptly ceased, and he heard moanings and sobbings as of a woman suffering from paroxysms of the most intense and violent grief. Combatting with a great fear that now began to seize him, he summed up the resolution to peep once more into the room, but though his eyes took in the whole range of the room, he could perceive no spot where anyone could possibly be in hiding, and nothing that would in any way account for the sounds. There was nothing in front of him but walls, furniture, and—space. Not a living creature. What then caused those sounds? He was asking himself this question, when the door opened, and Mr McMahon, followed by Katherine and all of the other girls, came into the apartment; and, with their entry, the strange sounds at once ceased.

"Why, what's the matter, Mr O'Farrell," the girls said, laughingly. "You are as white as a sheet and trembling all over. You haven't seen a ghost, have you?"

"I haven't seen anything," O'Farrell retorted, a trifle nettled at their gaiety, "but I've heard some rather extraordinary sounds."

"Extraordinary sounds," Katherine laughed. "What on earth do you mean?"

"Just what I say," O'Farrell remarked. "When I was on the veranda just now I distinctly heard the sound of a harp in this room, and shortly afterwards I heard a woman weeping."

"It must have been someone outside in the street," Mr McMahon observed hastily, at the same time giving O'Farrell a warning glance from his dark and penetrating eyes. "We do occasionally receive visits from street musicians. I have something to say to you about the English and their rumoured new attack on the town," and drawing O'Farrell aside he whispered to him: "On no account refer to that music again. It was undoubtedly the Banshee, the ghost that my forefathers brought over from Ireland, and it is only heard before some very dreadful catastrophe to the family."

The following day Badajoz was stormed and entered by the English, and in the wild scenes that ensued, scenes in which the drunken English soldiery got completely out of hands, many Spanish—Spanish men and women—perished, as well as French, and among the casualties were the entire McMahon family.

CHAPTER IX

THE BANSHEE AT SEA

Talking of phantom music, there is a widespread belief among Celtic races that whenever it is heard proceeding from the sea, either a death or some other great calamity is prognosticated. Such a belief is very prevalent along the coasts of Scotland, Wales, and Cornwall, and Mr Dyer, in his "Ghost World," p. 413, refers to it in Ireland. "Sometimes," he says, "music is heard at sea, and it is believed in Ireland that, when a friend or relative dies, a warning voice is discernible." To what extent this music is connected with Banshee hauntings it is, of course, impossible to say; but I have known cases in which it has owed its origin to the Banshee and to the Banshee only.

During the Civil War in America, for example, a transport of Confederate soldiers was making for Charlestown one evening, when a young Irish officer, who was leaning over the bulwarks and gazing pensively into the sea, was astonished to hear the very sweetest sounds of music coming from, so it seemed to him, the very depths of the blue waters. Thinking he must be dreaming, he called a brother officer to his side and asked him if he could hear anything.

"Yes," the latter responded, "music, and what is more, singing. It is a woman, and she is singing some very tender and plaintive air. How the deuce do you account for it?"

"I don't know," the young Irishman replied, "unless it is the Banshee, and it sounds very like the description of it that my mother used to give me. I only hope it does not predict the death of any one of my very near relatives."

It did not do that, but oddly enough, and unknown to him at the time, a namesake of his, whom he subsequently discovered was a second cousin, stood not ten yards from him at the very moment he was listening to the music, and was killed in action in a sortie from Charlestown on the following day.

A story of a similar nature was told me in Oregon by an old Irish Federal soldier, who was in the temporary employ of an apple merchant at Medford, Jackson County. I don't in any way vouch for its truth, but give it just as it was related to me.

"You ask me if I have ever come across any ghosts in America. Well, I guess I have, several, and amongst others the Banshee. Oh, yes, I am Irish, although I speak with the nasal twang of the regular Yank. Everyone does who has lived in the Eastern States for any length of time. It's the climate. My name, however, is

O'Hagan, and I was born in County Clare; and though my father was only a peasant, I'm a darned sight more Irish than half the people who possess titles and big estates in the old country to-day.

"I emigrated from Ireland with my parents, when I was only a few weeks old, and we settled in New York, where I was working as a porter on the quays when the Civil War broke out. Like me, the majority of Irishmen who, as you know, are always ready to go wherever there's the chance of doing a bit of fighting, I at once enlisted in the Marines, for I was passionately fond of the sea, and in due course of time was transferred to a gunboat that patrolled the Carolina Coast on the lookout for Confederate blockade runners. Well, one night, shortly after I had turned in and was lying in my hammock, trying to get to sleep, which was none too easy, for one of my mates, an ex-actor, was snoring loud enough to wake the whole ship, I suddenly heard a tapping on the porthole close beside me. 'Hello,' says I to myself, 'that's an odd noise. It can't be the water, nor yet the wind; maybe it's a bird, a gull or albatross,' and I listened very attentively. The sound went on, but it had none of that hardness and sharpness about it that is occasioned by a beak, it was softer and more lingering, more like the tapping of fingers. Every now and then it left off, to go on again, tap, tap, tap, until, at last, it unnerved me to such an extent that I jumped out of my hammock and had a peep to see what it was. To my astonishment I saw a very white face pressed against the porthole, looking in at me. It was the face of a woman with raven black hair that fell in long ringlets about her neck and shoulders. She had big golden rings in her ears, that shone like anything as the moonbeams caught them, as did her teeth, too, which were the loveliest bits of ivory I have ever seen, absolutely even and without the slightest mar.

"But it was her eyes that fascinated me most. They were large, not too large, however, but in strict proportion to the rest of her face, and as far as I could judge in the moonlight, either blue or grey, but indescribably beautiful, and, at the same time, indescribably sad. As I drew nearer, she shrank back, and pointed with a white and slender hand at a spot on the sea, and then suddenly I heard music, the far-away sound of a harp, proceeding, so it seemed to me, from about the place she had indicated. It was a very still night, and the sounds came to me very distinctly, above the soft lap, lap of the water against the vessel's side, and the mechanical squish, squish made by the bows each time they rose and fell, as the ship gently ploughed her way onwards. I was so intent on listening that I quite forgot the figure of the woman with the beautiful face, and when I turned to look at her again, she had gone, and there was nothing in front of me but an endless expanse of heaving, tossing, moonlit water. Then the music ceased, too, and all was still again, wondrously still, and feeling unaccountably sad and lonely—for I had taken a great fancy to that woman's face, the only what you might term really lovely woman's face that had ever looked kindly on me—I got back again into my hammock, and was soon fast asleep. On my touching at port, the first letter I received from home informed me of the death of my father, who had died the same night and just about the same time I had seen that fairy vision and heard that fairy music.

"When I told my mother about it, some long time afterwards, she said it was the Banshee, and that it had haunted the O'Hagan family for hundreds and hundreds of years."

This, as I have already said, is merely a trooper's story, unconfirmed by anyone else's evidence, and, of course, not up to the standard of S.P.R. authority. Yet, I believe, it was related to me in perfect sincerity, and the narrator had nothing whatever to gain through making it up. I did not even offer him a chew of tobacco, for at that moment I was pretty nearly, if not, indeed, quite as hard up as he was himself.

And now, before I finish altogether with Banshee hauntings that are associated with war, I feel I must refer to a statement in Mr McAnnaly's book, "Irish Wonders," to the effect that when the Duke of Wellington died, the Banshee was heard wailing round the house of his ancestors. This statement does not, in my opinion, bear inspection. I am quite ready to grant that some kind of apparition—perhaps a family ghost he had inherited from one or other of his Anglo-Irish ancestry—was heard lamenting outside the domain in question; but as the family to whom the Duke belonged could not be said to be of even anything approaching ancient Irish extraction, I cannot conceive it possible that the disturbances experienced were in any way due to the genuine Banshee.

To revert to the sea, and Banshee haunting. On the coast of Donegal there is an estuary called "The Rosses," and this at one time was said to be haunted by several kinds of phantoms, including the Banshee, which was reported to have manifested itself on quite a number of occasions.

Under the heading of "An Irish Water-fiend," Bourke, in his "Anecdotes of the Aristocracy" (i. 329), relates the following case of a ghostly happening there, which, although not due to a Banshee, is so characteristic of Irish supernatural phenomena that I cannot refrain from quoting it.

In the autumn of 1777 the Rev. James Crawford, rector of the parish of Killina, County Leitrim, was riding on horseback with his sister-in-law, Miss Hannah Wilson, on a pillion behind him, along the road leading to the "The Rosses," and, on reaching the estuary, he at once proceeded to cross it. After they had gone some distance, Miss Wilson, noticing that the water touched the saddle laps, became so alarmed that she cried out and besought Mr Crawford to turn the horse round and get back to land as quickly as possible.

"I do not think there can be danger," Mr Crawford answered, "for I see a horseman crossing the ford not twenty yards before us."

To this Miss Wilson, who also saw the horseman, replied:

"You had better hail him and inquire the depth of the intervening water."

Mr Crawford at once did so, whereupon the horseman stopped and, turning round, revealed a face distorted by the most hideous grin conceivable, and so frightfully white and evil that the luckless clergyman promptly beat a retreat, and made no attempt to check the mad haste of his panicked steed till he had left the estuary many miles behind him.

On arriving home he narrated the incident to his wife and family, and subsequently learned that the estuary was well known to be haunted by several phantoms, whose mission was invariably the same, either to foretell the doom by drowning of the person to whom they appeared, or else to actually bring about the death of that person by luring them on and on, until they got out of their depth, and so perished.

One would have thought that Mr Crawford, after the experience just narrated, would have given the estuary a very wide berth in future; but no such thing. He again attempted to cross the ford of "The Rosses" on 27th September, 1777, and was drowned in the endeavour.

Among many thrilling and (so it struck me at the time) authentic stories told me in my youth by a Mrs Broderick, a well-known vendor of oranges and chocolate in Bristol, were several stirring accounts of the Banshee. I was at the time a day boy at Clifton College, residing not very far from the school, and Mrs Broderick, who used to visit our house every week with her wares, took a particular interest in me because I was Irish—one of "the real old O'Donnells." She was a native of Cork, and had, I believe, migrated from that city in the *Juno*, an old cattle boat, that for more than twenty years plied regularly every week between Cork and Bristol carrying a handful of passengers, who, for the cheapness of the fare, made the best of the rolling and tossing and extremely limited space allotted for their accommodation. In later years I often travelled to and from Dublin and Bristol in the *Argo*, the *Juno's* sister ship, so I speak feelingly and from experience. But to proceed with Mrs Broderick's Banshee stories.

The one containing an account of a Banshee haunting on the sea I will narrate in this chapter, and the other, which has no connection with either sea or river, I will deal with later on.

Before I commence either story, however, I would like to say that though Mrs Broderick spoke with a rich brogue and was really Irish, she used few, if any, of those words and expressions that certain professors of the Dublin Academic School apparently consider inseparable from the speech of the Irish peasant class. I cannot, for example, remember her ever saying Musha, or Arrah, or Oro; and, as for Erse, I am quite certain she did not know a word of it. Yet, as I have said, she was Irish, and far more Irish than many of the Gaelic scholars of to-day who, insufferably proud of their knowledge of the Celtic tongue, bore one stiff by their feeble and futile attempts to acquire something of the real Irish wit and proverbial humour.

Mrs Broderick did not often speak of her parents; they were, I fancy, peasants, or, perhaps, what we should term "small farmers," and from what I could gather they lived, at one time, in a little village just outside Cork; but Mrs Broderick was, she told me, very fond of the sea, and often, when a girl, walked into Cork and went out boating with her young friends in Queenstown harbour.

On one occasion, she and another girl and two young men went for a sail with an old fisherman they knew, who took them some distance up the coast in the direction of Kinsale. There had been a slight breeze when they started, but it dropped suddenly as they were tacking to come back home, and since the sails had to be taken down and oars used, both the young men volunteered to row.

Their offer being accepted by the old fisherman, they pulled away steadily till they espied an old ship, so battered and worn away as to be little more than a mere shell, lying half in and half out of the water in a tiny cove. Then, as the weather was beautifully fine and no one was in a hurry to get home, it was proposed that they pull up to the wreck and examine it. The old fisherman demurred, but he was soon won over, and the two young men and Mrs Broderick's girl friend boarded the old hulk, leaving Mrs Broderick and the old fisherman in the boat. The shadows from the trees and rocks had already manifested themselves on the glistening shingles of the beach, and a glow, emanating from the rapidly rising moon and myriads of scintillating stars that every moment shone forth with increased brilliancy, showed up every object around them with startling distinctness.

Always in her element in scenes of this description, Mrs Broderick was enjoying herself to the utmost. Leaning on the side of the boat and trailing one hand in the water, she drank in the fresh night air, redolent with the scent of flowers and ozone. She could hear her friends talking and laughing as they tried to steady themselves on the sloping boards of the old hulk; and presently, one of them, O'Connell, proposed that they should descend below deck and explore the cabins. Then their voices gradually grew fainter and fainter, until eventually all was still, save for the lapping of the sea against the sides of the boat, and the gentle ripple of the wavelets as they broke on the beach, and the occasional far-away barkings of a dog—noises that somehow seem to belong to summer more than to any other period of the year.

Mrs Broderick's memory, awakened by these sounds, travelled back to past seasons, and she was depicting some of the old scenes over again, when all at once, from the wreck, from that side of it, so it seemed to her, that was partly under water, there rang out a series of the most appalling screams, just like the screams of a woman who had been suddenly pounced upon and either stabbed, or treated in some equally savage and violent manner.

Mrs Broderick, of course, at once thought of her friend, Mary Rooney, and, clutching the boatman by the arm, she exclaimed:

"The Saints above, it's Mary. They're murdering her."

"'Tis no woman, that," the old boatman said hoarsely. "'Tis the Banshee, and I would not have had this have happened for the whole blessed world. I with my mother so ill in bed with the rheumatism and a cold she got all through her with sitting out on the wet grass the night before last."

"Are you sure?" Mrs Broderick whispered, clutching him tighter, whilst her teeth chattered. "Are you sure it isn't Mary, and they are not killing her?"

"Sure," replied the boatman, "that's the way the Banshee always screams—'tis her, right enough, 'tis no human woman," and like the good Catholic that he was, he crossed himself, and, dipping the oars gently into the water, he began to pull slowly and quietly away.

By and by the screaming ceased, and a moment later the three explorers came trooping on to the deck, showing no signs whatever of alarm, and when questioned as to whether they had heard anything, laughingly replied in the negative.

"Only," O'Connell added facetiously, "the kiss Mike Power stole from Mary. That was all."

But for O'Connell that was not all. When he arrived home he found that during his absence his mother had died suddenly, and, in all probability, at the very moment when Mrs Broderick and the boatman had heard the Banshee.

CHAPTER X

ALLEGED COUNTERPARTS OF THE BANSHEE

No country besides Ireland possesses a Banshee, though some countries possess a family or national ghost somewhat resembling it. In Germany, for example, popular tradition is full of rumours of white ladies who haunt castles, woods, rivers, and mountains, where they may be seen combing their yellow hair, or playing on harps or spinning. They usually, as their name would suggest, wear white dresses, and not infrequently yellow or green shoes of a most dainty and artistic design. Sometimes they are sad, sometimes gay; sometimes they warn people of approaching death or disaster, and sometimes, by their beauty, they blind men to an impending peril, and thus lure them on to their death. When beautiful, they are often very beautiful, though nearly always of the same type—golden hair and long blue eyes; they are rarely dark, and their hair is never of that peculiar copper and golden hue that is so common among Banshees. When ugly, they are generally ugly indeed—either repulsive old crones, not unlike the witches in Grimm's Fairy Tales, or death-heads mockingly arrayed in the paraphernalia of the young; but their ugliness does not seem to embrace that ghastly satanic mockery, that diabolical malevolence that is inseparable from the malignant form of Banshee, and which inspires in the beholders such a peculiar and unparalleled horror.

It is not my intention in this work to do more than briefly refer to a few of the most famous of the German hauntings in their relation to the Banshee; and, since it is the best known, I would first of all call attention to the White Lady, that restricts its unwelcome attentions to Royalty, and more especially, perhaps, to that branch of it known as the House of Hohenzollern. Between this White Lady family phantasm and the Banshee there is undoubtedly something in common. They are both exclusively associated with families of really ancient lineage, which they follow about from town to town, province to province, and country to country; and the purpose of their respective missions is generally the same, namely, to give warning of some approaching death or calamity, which in the case of the White Lady is usually of a national order.

Occasionally, too, the German family ghost, like the Banshee, is heard playing on a harp, but here I think the likeness ends. There are no very striking characteristics in the appearance of the White Lady of the Hohenzollerns, she would seem to be neither very beautiful nor the reverse; nor does she convey the impression of belonging to any very remote age; on the contrary, she might well be the earthbound spirit of someone who died in the Middle Ages or even later.

In December, 1628, she was seen in the Royal Palace in Berlin, and was heard to say, *"Veni, judica vivos et mortuos; judicum mihi adhuc superest"* —that is to say, "Come judge the quick and the dead—I wait for judgment." She also manifested herself to one of the Fredericks of Prussia, who regarded her advent as a sure sign of his approaching death, which it was, for he died shortly afterwards. We next read of her appearing in Bohemia at the Castle of Neuhaus. One of the princesses of the royal house was trying on a new head-gear before a mirror, and, thinking her waiting-maid was near at hand, she inquired of her the time. To the Princess's horror, however, instead of the maid answering her, a strange figure all in white, which her instincts told her was the famous national ghost, stepped out from behind a screen and exclaimed, *"Zehn uhr ist es irh Liebden!"* "It is ten o'clock, your love"; the last two words being the mode of address usually adopted in Germany and Austria by Royalties when speaking to one another. The Princess was soon afterwards taken ill and died.

A faithful account of the appearance of the White Lady was published in *The Iris*, a Frankfort journal, in 1829, and was vouched for by the editor, George Doring. Doring's mother, who was companion to one of the ladies at the Prussian Court, had two daughters, aged fourteen and fifteen, who were in the habit of visiting her at the Palace. On one occasion, when the two girls were alone in their mother's sitting-room, doing some needlework, they were immeasurably surprised to hear the sounds of music, proceeding, so it seemed to them, from behind a big stove that occupied one corner of the apartment. One girl got up, and, taking a yard measure, struck the spot where she fancied the music was coming from; whereupon the measure was instantly snatched from her hand, the music, at the same time, ceasing. She was so badly frightened that she ran out of the room and took refuge in someone else's apartment.

On her return some minutes later, she found her sister lying on the floor in a dead faint. On coming to, this sister stated that directly the other had quitted the apartment, the music had begun again and, not only that, but the figure of a woman, all in white, had suddenly risen from behind the stove and began to advance towards her, causing her instantly to faint with fright.

The lady in whose house the occurrence took place, on being acquainted with what had happened, had the flooring near the stove taken up; but, instead of discovering the treasure which she had hoped might be there, a quantity of quick-lime only was found; and the affair eventually getting to the King's ears, he displayed no surprise, but merely expressed his belief that the apparition the girl had seen was that of the Countess Agnes of Orlamunde, who had been bricked up alive in that room.

She had been the mistress of a former Margrave of Brandenburg, by whom she had had two children, and when the Margrave's legitimate wife died the Countess hoped he would marry her. This, however, he declined to do on the plea that her offspring, at his death, would very probably dispute the heirship to the property with the children of his lawful marriage. The Countess then, in order to remove this obstacle to her union, poisoned her two children, which act so disgusted the Margrave that he had her walled up alive in the room where she had committed the crimes. The King went on to explain that the phantasm appeared about every seven years, but more often to children, to whom it was believed to be very much attached, than to adults.

Against this explanation, however, is the more recent one that the White Lady is Princess Bertha or Perchta von Rosenberg. This theory is founded on the discovery of a portrait of Princess Bertha, which was identified by someone as the portrait of the White Lady whom they had just seen.

In support of this theory it was pointed out that once when certain charities which the Princess had stated in her will should be doled out annually to the poor were neglected, not only was the White Lady seen, but music and all kinds of other sounds were heard in the house where the Princess had died. Very possibly, however, in neither of these theories is there any truth, and the secret of the White Lady's activity lies in some subtle and, perhaps, entirely unsuspected fact. It is, I think, quite conceivable that she is no earth-bound soul, but some impersonating elemental, which—like the Banshee—has, for some strange and wholly inexplicable reason, attached itself to the unfortunate Hohenzollerns, and their relatives and kinsmen.

Ballinus and Erasmus Francisci, in their published works, give numerous accounts of the appearance of this same apparition; whilst Mrs Crowe asserts that it was seen shortly before the publication of her "Night Side of Nature." It would be interesting to know whether it appeared to the ex-Kaiser Wilhelm, or to any of his family, before this last greatest and most signally disastrous of all wars.

William Brereton in his "Travels" (i. 33) gives rather a different description of this ghost. He says that the Queen of Bohemia told him "that at Berlin—the Elector of Brandenberg's house—before the death of anyone related in blood to that house, there appears and walks up and down that house like unto a ghost in a white sheet, which walks during the time of their sickness until their death."

In this account it will be noticed that there is no mention of sex, so that the reader can only speculate as to whether the apparition was the ghost of a man or a woman. Its appearance, however, according to this account, strongly suggests a ghost of the sepulchral and death-head type—an ordinary species of elemental—which suggestion is not apparent in any other description of it that we have hitherto come across. Other ancient German and Austrian families, besides those of the ruling houses, possess their family ghosts, and here again, as in the parallel case of the Irish and their Banshee, the family ghost of the Germans or Austrians is by no means confined to the "White Lady." In some cases of German family haunting, for example, the phenomenon is a roaring lion, in others a howling dog; and in others a bell or gong, or sepulchral toned clock striking at some unusual hour, and generally thirteen times. In all instances, however, no matter whether the family ghost be German, Irish, or Austrian, the purpose of its manifestations is the same—to predict death or some very grave calamity.[12]

In the notes to the 1844 edition of Thomas Crofton Croker's "Fairy Legends and Traditions of the South of Ireland," we find this paragraph taken from the

---

[12] See "The Ghost World," by T. F. T. Dyer, p. 227.

works of the Brothers Grimm and manuscript communications from Dr Wilhelm Grimm:

"In the Tyrol they believe in a spirit which looks in at the window of a house in which a person is to die (Deutsche Sagen, No. 266), the White Woman with a veil over her head answers to the Banshee, but the tradition of the Klage-weib (mourning woman) in the Lünchurger Heath (Spiels Archiv. ii. 297) resembles it more. On stormy nights, when the moon shines faintly through the fleeting clouds, she stalks of gigantic stature with death-like aspect, and black, hollow eyes, wrapt in grave clothes which float in the wind, and stretches her immense arm over the solitary hut, uttering lamentable cries in the tempestuous darkness. Beneath the roof over which the Klage-weib has leaned, one of the inmates must die in the course of a month."

In Italy there are several families of distinction possessing a family ghost that somewhat resembles the Banshee. According to Cardau and Henningius Grosius the ancient Venetian family of Donati possess a ghost in the form of a man's head, which is seen looking through a doorway whenever any member of the family is doomed to die. The following extract from their joint work serves as an illustration of it:

"Jacopo Donati, one of the most important families in Venice, had a child, the heir to the family, very ill. At night, when in bed, Donati saw the door of his chamber opened and the head of a man thrust in. Knowing that it was not one of his servants, he roused the house, drew his sword, went over the whole palace, all the servants declaring that they had seen such a head thrust in at the doors of their several chambers at the same hour; the fastenings were found all secure, so that no one could have come in from without. The next day the child died."

Other families in Italy, a branch of the Paoli, for example, is haunted by very sweet music, the voice of a woman singing to the accompaniment of a harp or guitar, and invariably before a death.

Of the family ghost in Spain I have been able to gather but little information. There, too, some of the oldest families seem to possess ghosts that follow the fortunes, both at home and abroad, of the families to which they are attached, but with the exception of this one point of resemblance there seems to be in them little similarity to the Banshee.

In Denmark and Sweden the likeness between the family ghost and the Banshee is decidedly pronounced. Quite a number of old Scandinavian families possess attendant spirits very much after the style of the Banshee; some very beautiful and sympathetic, and some quite the reverse; the most notable difference being that in the Scandinavian apparition there is none of that ghastly mixture of the grave, antiquity, and hell that is so characteristic of the baleful type of Banshee, and which would seem to distinguish it from the ghosts of all other countries. The beautiful Scandinavian phantasms more closely resemble fairies or angels than any women of this earth, whilst the hideous ones have all the grotesqueness and crude horror of the witches of Andersen or Grimm. There is nothing about them, as there so often is in the Banshee, to make one wonder if they can be the phantasms of any long extinct race, or people, for example, that might have hailed from the missing continent of Atlantis, or have been in Ireland prior to the coming of the Celts.

The Scandinavian family ghosts are frankly either elementals or the earthbound spirits of the much more recent dead. Yet, as I have said, they have certain points in common with the Banshee. They prognosticate death or disaster; they scream and wail like women in the throes of some great mental or physical agony; they sob or laugh; they occasionally tap on the window-panes, or play on the harp; they sometimes haunt in pairs, a kind spirit and an evilly disposed one attending the fortunes of the same family; and they keep exclusively to the very oldest families. Oddly enough at times the Finnish family ghost assumes the guise of a man. Burton, for example, in his "Anatomy of Melancholy," tells us "that near Rufus Nova, in Finland, there is a lake in which, when the governor of the castle dies, a spectrum is seen in the habit of Orion, with a harp, and makes excellent music, like those clocks in Cheshire which (they say) presage death to the masters of the family; or that oak in Lanthadran Park in Cornwall, which foreshadows so much."

I will not dwell any longer, however, on Scandinavian ghosts, as I purpose later on to publish a volume on the same, but will pass on to the family apparitions of Scotland, England, and Wales.

Beginning with Scotland, Sir Walter Scott was strong in his belief in the Banshee, which he described as one of the most beautiful superstitions of Europe. In his "Letters on Demonology" he says: "Several families of the Highlands of Scotland anciently laid claim to the distinction of an attendant spirit, who performed the office of the Irish Banshee," and he particularly referred to the ghostly cries and lamentations which foreboded death to members of the Clan of MacLean of Lochbery. But though many of the Highland families do possess such a ghost, unlike the Banshee, it is not restricted to the feminine sex, nor does its origin, as a rule, date back to anything like such remote times. It would seem, indeed, to belong to a much more ordinary species of phantasm, a species which is seldom accompanied by music or any other sound, and which by no means always prognosticates death, although on many occasions it has done so.

In addition to the MacLean, some of the best known cases of Scottish family ghosts are as follows:

The Bodach au Dun, or Ghost of the Hills, which haunts the family of Grant Rothiemurcus, and the Llam-dearg, or spectre of the Bloody Hand, which pursues the fortunes of the Clan Kinchardine. According to Sir Walter Scott in the Macfarlane MSS. this spirit was chiefly to be seen in the Glenmore, where it took the form of a soldier with one hand perpetually dripping with blood. At one time it invariably signalled its advent in the manner which, I think, has no parallel among ghosts—it challenged members of the Kinchardine Clan to fight a duel with it, and whether they accepted or not they always died soon afterwards. As lately as 1669, says Sir Walter Scott, it fought with three brothers, one after another, who immediately died therefrom.

Then there is the Clan of Gurlinbeg which is haunted by Garlin Bodacher; the

Turloch Gorms who, according to Scott, are haunted by Mary Moulach, or the girl with the hairy left hand[13]; and the Airlie family, whose seat at Cortachy is haunted by the famous drummer, whose ghostly tattoos must be taken as a sure sign that a member of the Ogilvie Clan—of which the Earl of Airlie is the recognised head—will die very shortly.

Mr Ingram, in his "Haunted Houses and Family Legends," quotes several well authenticated instances of manifestations by this apparition, the last occurring, according to him, in the year 1899, though I have heard from other reliable sources that it has been heard at a much more recent date. The origin of this haunting is generally thought to be comparatively modern, and not to date further back than two or three hundred years, if as far, which, of course, puts it on quite a different category from that of the Banshee, though its mission is, without doubt, the same. According to Mr Ingram, a former Lord Airlie, becoming jealous of one of his retainers or emissaries who was a drummer, had him thrust in his drum and hurled from a top window of the castle into the courtyard beneath, where he was dashed to pieces. With his dying breath the drummer cursed not only Lord Airlie, but his descendants, too, and ever since that event his apparition has persistently haunted the family.

Other Highland families that possess special ghosts are a branch of the Macdonnells, that have a phantom piper, whose mournful piping invariably means that some member or other of the clan is shortly doomed to die; and the Stanleys who have a female apparition that signalises her advent by shrieking, weeping, and moaning before the death of any of the family. Perhaps of all Scottish ghosts this last one most closely resembles the Banshee, though there are distinct differences, chiefly with regard to the appearance of the phantoms—the Scottish one differing essentially in her looks and attire from the Irish ghost—and their respective origins, that of the Stanley apparition being, in all probability, of much later date than the Banshee.

Then, again, there is the Bodach Glas, or dark grey man, in reference to which Mr Henderson, in his "Folk-lore of Northern Countries," p. 344, says: "Its appearance foretold death in the Clan of — —, and I have been informed on the most credible testimony of its appearance in our own day. The Earl of E— —, a nobleman alike beloved and respected in Scotland, was playing on the day of his decease on the links of St Andrew's at golf. Suddenly he stopped in the middle of the game, saying, 'I can play no longer, there is the Bodach Glas. I have seen it for the third time; something fearful is going to befall me.' That night he fell down dead as he was giving a lady her candlestick on her way up to bed."

Another instance, still, of a Scottish family ghost is that of the willow tree at Gordon Castle, which is referred to by Sir Bernard Bourke in his "Anecdotes of the Aristocracy." Sir Bernard asserts that whenever any accident happens to this tree, if, for example, a branch is blown down in a storm, or any part of it is struck by lightning, then some dire misfortune is sure to happen to some member of the family.

---

[13] See Sir Walter Scott's Poetical Works, 1853, VIII., p. 126.

There are other old Scottish family ghosts, all very distinct from the Banshee, though a few bear some slight resemblance to it, but as my space is restricted, I will pass on to family ghosts of a more or less similar type that are to be met with in England.

To begin with, the Oxenhams of Devonshire the heiress of Sir James Oxenham, and the bride that is invariably seen before the death of any member of the family. According to a well-known Devonshire ballad, a bird answering to this description flew over the guests at the wedding of the heiress of Sir James Oxenham, and the bride was killed the following day by a suitor she had unceremoniously jilted.

The Arundels of Wardour have a ghost in the form of two white owls, it being alleged that whenever two birds of this species are seen perched on the house where any of this family are living, some one member of them is doomed to die very shortly.

Equally famous is the ghost of the Cliftons of Nottinghamshire, which takes the shape of a sturgeon that is seen swimming in the river Trent, opposite Clifton Hall, the chief seat of the family, whenever one of the Cliftons is on the eve of dying.

Then, again, there is the white hand of the Squires of Worcestershire, a family that is now practically extinct. According to local tradition this family was for many generations haunted by the very beautiful hand of a woman, that was always seen protruding through the wall of the room containing that member of the family who was fated to die soon. Most ghost hands are said to be grey and filmy, but this one, according to some eye-witnesses, appears to have borne an extraordinary resemblance to that of a living person. It was slender and perfectly proportioned, with very tapering fingers and very long and beautifully kept filbert nails—the sort of hand one sees in portraits of women of bygone ages, but which one very rarely meets with in the present generation.

Other families that possess ghosts are the Yorkshire Middletons, who are always apprised of the death of one of their members by the appearance of a nun; and the Byrons of Newstead Abbey, who, according to the great poet of that name, were haunted by a black Friar that used to be seen wandering about the cloisters and other parts of the monasterial building before the death of any member of the family.

In England, there seems to be quite a number of White Lady phantoms, most of them, however, haunting houses and not families, and none of them bearing any resemblance to the Banshee. Indeed, there is a far greater dissimilarity between the English and Irish types of family ghosts than there is between the Irish and those of any of the nations I have hitherto discussed.

Lastly, with regard to the Welsh family ghosts, Mr Wirt Sikes, in his "British Goblins," quite erroneously, I think, likens the Banshee in appearance to the Gwrach y Rhibyn, or Hag of the Dribble, which he describes as hideous, with long, black teeth, long, lank, withered arms, leathern wings, and cadaverous cheeks, a description that is certainly not in the least degree like that of any Banshee I have ever heard of. He goes on to add that it comes in the stillness of the night, utters a blood-curdling howl, and calls on the person doomed to die thus: "Da-a-a-vy! De-i-i-o-o-ba-a-a-ch." If it is in the guise of a male it says, in addition, "Fy mlentyn, fy mlentyn bach!" which rendered into English is, "My child, my little child"; but if in the form of a woman, "Oh! Oh! fy ngwr, fy ngwr" — "My husband! my husband!" As a rule it flaps its wings against the window of the room in which the person who is doomed is sleeping, whilst occasionally it appears either to the ill-fated one himself or to some member of his family in a mist on the mountainside.

Mr Sikes gives a very graphic description of the appearance of this apparition to a peasant farmer near Cardiff, a little over forty years ago. To be precise, it was on the evening of the 14th November, 1877. The farmer was on a visit to an old friend at the time, and was awakened at midnight by the most ghastly screaming and a violent shaking of the window-frame. The noise continued for some seconds, and then terminated in one final screech that far surpassed all the others in intensity and sheer horror. Greatly excited — though Mr Sikes affirms he was not frightened — the old man leaped out of bed, and, throwing open the window, saw a figure like a frightful old woman, with long, dishevelled, red hair, and tusk-like teeth, and a startling white complexion, floating in mid-air. She was enveloped in a long, loose, flowing kind of black robe that entirely concealed her body. As he gazed at her, completely dumbfounded with astonishment, she peered down at him and, throwing back her dreadful head, emitted another of the very wildest and most harrowing of screams. He then heard her flap her wings against a window immediately underneath his, after which he saw her fly over to an inn almost directly opposite him, called the "Cow and Snuffers," and pass right through the closed doorway.

After waiting some minutes to see if she came out again, he at length got back into bed, and on the morrow learned that Mr Llewellyn, the landlord of the "Cow and Snuffers," had died in the night about the same time as the apparition, which he, the old farmer, now concluded must have been the Gwrach y Rhibyn, had appeared.

There is, of course, this much in common between the Gwrach y Rhibyn and the Banshee: both are harbingers of death; both signalise their advent by shrieks, and both confine their hauntings to really ancient Celtic families; but here, it seems to me, the likeness ends. The Gwrach y Rhibyn is more grotesque than horrible, and would seem to belong rather to the order of witches in fairy lore than to the denizens of the ghost world.

Another ghostly phenomenon of the death-warning type that is, I believe, to be met with in Wales, is the Canhywllah Cyrth, or corpse candle, so called because the apparition resembles a material candlelight, saving for the fact that it vanishes directly it is approached, and reforms speedily again afterwards. The following descriptions of the Canhywllah Cyrth are taken from Mr T. C. Charley's "News from the Invisible World," pp. 121-4. The first extract is the account of the corpse candles given by the Rev. Mr Davis.

"If it be a little candle," he writes, "pale or bluish, then follows the corpse either of an abortive, or some infant; if a big one, then the corpse either of someone come of age; if there be seen two or three or more, some big, some small, together, then so many such corpses together. If two candles come from divers places, and be seen to meet, the corpses will do the like; if any of these candles be seen to turn, sometimes a little out of the way that leadeth unto the church, the following corpse will be found to turn into that very place, for the avoiding of some dirty lane, etc. When I was about fifteen years of age, dwelling at Llanglar, late at night, some neighbours saw one of these candles hovering up and down along the bank of the river, until they were weary in beholding; at last they left it so, and went to bed. A few weeks after, a damsel from Montgomeryshire came to see her friends, who dwelt on the other side of the Istwyth, and thought to ford it at the place where the light was seen; but being dissuaded by some lookers-on (by reason of a flood) she walked up and down along the bank, where the aforesaid candle did, waiting for the falling of the waters, which at last she took, and was drowned therein."

Continuing, he says: "Of late, my sexton's wife, an aged understanding woman, saw from her bed a little bluish candle upon her table; within two or three days after comes a fellow in, inquiring for her husband, and taking something from under his cloak, clapped it down directly upon the table end, where she had seen the candle; and what was it but a dead-born child?"

In another case the same gentleman relates a number of these candles were seen together. "About thirty-four or thirty-five years since," he says, "one Jane Wyat, my wife's sister, being nurse to Baronet Reid's three eldest children, and (the lady being deceased) the lady controller of that house, going late into a chamber where the maidservants lay, saw there no less than five of these lights together. It happened a while after, the chamber being newly plastered and a great grate of coal-fire thereon kindled to hasten the drying up of the plastering, that five of the maidservants went there to bed, as they were wont, but in the morning they were all dead, being suffocated in their sleep with the steam of the newly tempered lime and coal. This was at Llangathen in Carmarthenshire."

Occasionally a figure is seen with the lights, but nearly always that of a woman. À propos of this the same writer says: "William John of the County of Carmarthen, a smith, on going home one night, saw one of the corpse candles; he went out of his way to meet with it, and when he came near it, he saw it was a burying; and the corpse upon the bier, the perfect resemblance of a woman in the neighbourhood whom he knew, holding the candle between her forefingers, who dreadfully grinned at him, and presently he was struck down from his horse, where he remained a while, and was ill a long time after before he recovered. This was before the real burying of the woman. His fault, and therefore his danger, was his coming presumptuously against the candle."

Lastly, an account of these death candles appeared some years ago in *Fraser's Magazine*. It ran as follows:

"In a wild and retired district in North Wales, the following occurrence took place to the great astonishment of the mountaineers. We can vouch for the truth of the statement, as many members of our own teutu, or clan, were witnesses of the fact. On a dark evening, a few winters ago, some persons, with whom we are well acquainted, were returning to Barmouth, on the south or opposite side of the river. As they approached the ferryhouse at Penthryn, which is directly opposite Barmouth, they observed a light near the house, which they conjectured to be produced by a bonfire, and greatly puzzled they were to discover the reason why it should have been lighted. As they came nearer, however, it vanished; and when they inquired at the house respecting it, they were surprised to learn that not only had the people there displayed no light, but they had not even seen one; nor could they perceive any signs of it on the sands. On reaching Barmouth, the circumstance was mentioned, and the fact corroborated by some of the people there, who had also plainly and distinctly seen the light. It was settled, therefore, by some of the old fisherman, that this was a "death-token"; and, sure enough, the man who kept the ferry at that time was drowned at high-water a few nights afterwards, on the very spot where the light was seen. He was landing from the boat, when he fell into the water, and so perished."

"The same winter the Barmouth people, as well as the inhabitants of the opposite banks, were struck by the appearance of a number of small lights which were seen dancing in the air at a place called Borthwyn, about half a mile from the town. A great number of people came out to see these lights; and after a while they all but one disappeared, and this one proceeded slowly towards the water's edge, to a small bay where some boats were moored. The men in a sloop which was anchored near the spot saw the light advancing—they saw it also hover for a few seconds over one particular boat, and then totally disappear. Two or three days afterwards, the man to whom that particular boat belonged was drowned in the river, where he was sailing about Barmouth harbour in that very boat. We have narrated these facts just as they occurred."

Another well-known Welsh haunting that may be relegated to the same class of phenomena as the corpse candles is that of the Stradling Ghost. This phantasm, which is supposed to be that of a former Lady Stradling, who was murdered by one of her own relatives, haunts St Donart's Castle, on the southern coast of Glamorganshire, appearing whenever a death or some very grievous calamity is about to overtake a member of the family. Writing of her, Mr Wirt Sikes, in his "British Goblins," p. 143-4, says: "She appears when any mishap is about to befall a member of the house of Stradling, the direct line, however, of which is extinct. She wears high-heeled shoes, and a long trailing gown of the finest silk." According to local reports, her advent is always known in the neighbourhood by the behaviour of the dogs, which, taking their cue from their canine representatives in the Castle, begin to howl and whine, and keep on making a noise and showing every indication of terror and resentment so long as the earth-bound spirit of the lady continues to roam about. Of course the Stradling Ghost cannot be said to be characteristically Welsh, because its prototype is to be found in so many other countries, but it at least comes under the category of family apparitions.

The Gwyllgi, or dog of darkness, which Mr Wirt Sikes asserts has often inspired terror among the Welsh peasants, does not appear to be confined to any one family, any more than do the corpse candles, though, like the latter, it would seem to manifest itself principally to really Welsh people. Its advent is not, however, predicative of any special happening. The Cwn Annwn, or dogs of hell, that are chiefly to be met with in the south of Wales, on the contrary, rarely, if ever, appear, saving to warn those who see them of some approaching death or disaster. Neither they, nor the Gwyllgi, nor the corpse candles, since they do not haunt one family exclusively, can be called family ghosts. And only inasmuch as they are racial have they anything in common with the Banshee. Indeed, there is a world of difference between the Banshee and even its nearest counterpart in other countries, and the difference is, perhaps, one which only those who have actually experienced it could ever understand.

CHAPTER XI

THE BANSHEE IN POETRY AND PROSE

"'Twas the Banshee's lonely wailing,
Well I knew the voice of death,
On the night wind slowly sailing
O'er the bleak and gloomy heath."

These are the dramatic lines Thomas Crofton Croker, in his inimitable "Fairy Legends and Traditions of the South of Ireland," puts in the mouth of the widow MacCarthy, as she is lamenting over the body of her son, Charles, whose death had been predicted by the Banshee; not the beautiful and dainty Banshee of the O'Briens, but a wild, unkempt, haggish creature that seemed in perfect harmony with the drear and desolate moorland from whence it sprang.

Mr Croker, indeed, almost invariably associates the Banshee with the heath and bogland, for at the commencement of his Tales of the Banshee in the same volume, we find these well-known lines:

"Who sits upon the heath forlorn,
With robe so free and tresses worn,
Anon she pours a harrowing strain,
And then she sits all mute again!
Now peals the wild funereal cry,
And now—it sinks into a sigh."

Very different from this grim and repellent portrayal of the Banshee given by Mr Croker is the very pleasing and attractive description of it presented to us by Dr Kenealy, whose account of it in prose appears in an earlier chapter of this book.

Referring to the death of his brother, Dr Kenealy says:

"Here the Banshee, that phantom bright who weeps
Over the dying of her own loved line,
Floated in moonlight; in her streaming locks
Gleamed starshine; when she looked on me, she knew
And smiled."

And again:

"The wish has but
Escaped my lips—and lo! once more it streams
In liquid lapse upon the fairy winds
That guard each slightest note with jealous care,

And bring them hither, even as angels might
To the beloved to whom they minister."

In reference to phantom music heard at sea, Mr Dyer, in his "Ghost World," p. 413, quotes the following lines:

"A low sound of song from the distance I hear,
In the silence of night, breathing sad on my ear,
Whence comes it? I know not—unearthly the note,
Yet it sounds like the lay that my mother once sung,
As o'er her first-born in his cradle she hung."

As I have already stated, the Banshee is not infrequently heard at sea, either singing or weeping, hence, in all probability, the author of these lines, whose name, by the way, Mr Dyer does not divulge, had the Banshee in mind when he wrote them. But, perhaps, the best known, as well as the most direct reference to this ghost in verse is that made by Ireland's popular poet, Thomas Moore, in one of the most famous of his "Irish Melodies." I append the poem, not only for the reference it contains, but also on account of its general beauty.

"How oft has the Banshee cried!
How oft has death untied
Bright bonds that glory wove
Sweet bonds entwin'd by love.
Peace to each manly soul that sleepeth!
Rest to each faithful eye that weepeth!
Long may the fair and brave
Sigh o'er the hero's grave.

We're fallen upon gloomy days,
Star after star decays,
Every bright name, that shed
Light o'er the land, is fled.
Dark falls the tear of him who mourneth
Lost joy, a hope that ne'er returneth,
But brightly flows the tear
Wept o'er the hero's bier.

Oh, quenched are our beacon lights
Thou, of the hundred fights!
Thou, on whose burning tongue
Truth, peace, and freedom hung!
Both mute, but long as valour shineth
Or Mercy's soul at war refineth
So long shall Erin's pride
Tell how they lived and died."

With the following extracts from the translation of an elegy written by Pierse Ferriter, the Irish poet soldier, who fought bravely in the Cromwellian wars, I must now terminate these references to the Banshee in poetry:

"When I heard lamentations
And sad, warning cries
From the Banshees of many
Broad districts arise.
Aina from her closely hid
Nest did awake
The woman of wailing
From Gur's voicy lake;
From Glen Fogradh of words
Came a mournful whine,
And all Kerry's Banshees
Wept the lost Geraldine.[14]
The Banshees of Youghal
And of stately Mo-geely
Were joined in their grief
By wide Imokilly.
Carah Mona in gloom
Of deep sorrow appears,
And all Kinalmeaky's
Absorbed into tears.

.　　.　　.　　.

The Banshee of Dunquin
In sweet song did implore
To the spirit that watches
O'er dark Dun-an-oir,
And Ennismare's maid
By the dark, gloomy wave
With her clear voice did mourn
The fall of the brave.
On stormy Slieve Mish
Spread the cry far and wide,
From steeply Finnaleun
The wild eagle replied.
'Mong the Reeks, like the
Thunder peal's echoing rout,
It burst—and deep moaning
Bright Brandon gives out,
Oh Chief! whose example
On soft-minded youth
Like the signet impressed

[14] These extracts are taken from quotations of the poem in Chapter II. of a work entitled "Ancient History of the Kingdom of Kerry" by Friar O'Sullivan of Muckross Abbey, published in the Journal of the Cork Historical and Archæological Society (Vol. V., No. 44); and Friar O'Sullivan, in commenting upon these passages relating to the Banshees, writes (quoting from "Kerry Records"): "It seems that at this time it was the universal opinion that every district belonging to the Geraldines had its own attendant Banshee" (see *Archæological Journal*, 1852, on "Folk Lore" by N. Kearney).

Honour, glory, and truth.
The youth who once grieved
If unnoticed passed by,
Now deplore thee in silence
With sorrow-dimmed eye,
O! woman of tears,
Who, with musical hands,
From your bright golden hair
Hath combed out the long bands,
Let those golden strings loose,
Speak your thoughts—let your mind
Fling abroad its full light,
Like a torch to the wind."

In fiction no writer has, I think, dealt more freely with the subject of the Banshee than Thomas Crofton Croker, the translator of the abovementioned elegy. In his "Fairy Legends and Traditions of the South of Ireland," he gives the most inimitable accounts of it; and for the benefit of those of my readers who are unacquainted with his works, as well as for the purpose of presenting the Banshee as seen by such an unrivalled portrayer of Irish ghost and fairy lore, I will give a brief résumé of two of his stories.

The one I will take first relates to the Rev. Charles Bunworth, who about the middle of the eighteenth century was rector of Buttevant, County Cork. Mr Bunworth was greatly beloved and esteemed, not only on account of his piety—for pious people are by no means always popular—but also on account of his charity. He used to give pecuniary aid, often when he could ill afford it, to all and any, no matter to what faith they belonged, whom he really believed were in need; and being particularly fond of music, especially the harp, he entertained, in a most generous and hospitable manner, all the poor Irish harpers that came to his house. At the time of his death, no fewer than fifteen harps were found in the loft of his granary, presents, one is led to infer, from strolling harpers, in token of their gratitude for his repeated acts of kindness to them.

About a week prior to his decease, and at an early hour in the evening, several of the occupants of his house heard a strange noise outside the hall door, which they could only liken to the shearing of sheep. No very serious attention, however, was paid to it, and it was not until some time afterwards, when other queer things happened, that it was recalled and associated with the supernatural. Later on, at about seven o'clock in the evening, Kavanagh, the herdman, returned from Mallow, whither he had been dispatched for some medicine. He appeared greatly agitated, and, in response to Miss Bunworth's questions as to what was the matter, could only ejaculate:

"The master, Miss, the master! He is going from us."

Miss Bunworth, thinking he had been drinking, sternly reproved him, whereupon he responded:

"Miss, as I hope mercy hereafter, neither bite nor sup has passed my lips since

I left this house; but the master— —" Here he broke down, only adding with an effort, "We will lose him—the master." He then began to weep and wring his hands.

Miss Bunworth, who, during this strange recital, was growing more and more bewildered, now exclaimed impatiently:

"What *is* it you mean? Do explain yourself."

Kavanagh was silent, but, as she persisted, commanding him to speak, he at length said:

"The Banshee has come for him, Miss; and 'tis not I alone who have heard her."

But Miss Bunworth only laughed and rebuked him for being superstitious.

"Maybe I am superstitious," he retorted, "but as I came through the glen of Ballybeg she was along with me, keening, and screeching, and clapping her hands by my side, every step of the way, with her long white hair falling about her shoulders, and I could hear her repeat the master's name every now and then, as plain as ever I hear it. When I came to Old Abby, she parted from me there, and turned into pigeon field next the berrin'-ground, and, folding her cloak about her, down she sat under the tree that was struck by lightning, and began keening so bitterly that it went through one's heart to hear it."

Miss Bunworth listened more attentively now, but told Kavanagh that she was sure he was mistaken, as her father was very much better and quite out of danger. However, she spoke too soon, for that very night her father had a relapse and was soon in a very critical condition. His daughters nursed him with the utmost devotion, but at length, overcome with the strain of many hours of sleepless watchfulness, they were obliged to take a rest and allow a certain old friend of theirs, temporarily, to take their place.

It was night; without the house everything was still and calm; within the aged watcher was seated close beside the sick man's bed, the head of which had been placed near the window, so that the sufferer could, in the daylight, steal a glimpse at the fields and trees he loved so much. In an adjoining room, and in the kitchen, were a number of friends and dependents who had come from afar to inquire after the condition of the patient. Their conversation had been carried on for some time in whispers, and then, as if infected by the intense hush outside, they had gradually ceased talking, and all had become absolutely hushed. Suddenly the aged watcher heard a sound outside the window. She looked, but though there was a brilliant moonlight, which rendered every object far and near strikingly conspicuous, she could perceive nothing—nothing at least that could account for the disturbance. Presently the noise was repeated; a rose tree near the window rustled and seemed to be pulled violently aside. Then there was the sound like the clapping of hands and of breathing and blowing close to the window-panes.

At this, the old watcher, who was now getting nervous, arose and went into the next room, and asked those assembled there if they had heard anything. Apparently, they had not, but they all went out and searched the grounds, particularly in the vicinity of the rose tree, but could discover no clue as to the cause of the noises, and although the ground was soft with recent rain, there were no footprints to be seen anywhere. After they had made an exhaustive examination, and had settled down again indoors, the clapping at once recommenced, and was accompanied this time by moanings, which the whole party of investigators now heard. The sounds went on for some time, apparently till close to dawn, when the reverend gentleman died.

The other story concerns the MacCarthys, of whom Mr Croker remarks, "being an old, and especially an old Catholic family, they have, of course, a Banshee."

Charles MacCarthy in 1749 was the only surviving son of a very numerous family. His father died when he was twenty, leaving him his estate, and being very gay, handsome, and thoughtless, he soon got into bad company and made an unenviable reputation for himself. Going from one excess to another he at length fell ill, and was soon in such a condition that his life was finally despaired of by the doctor. His mother never left him. Always at his bedside, ready to administer to his slightest want, she showed how truly devoted she was to him, although she was by no means blind to his faults. Indeed, so acutely did she realise the danger in which his soul stood, that she prayed most earnestly that should he die, he should at least be spared long enough to be able to recover sufficiently to see the enormity of his offences, and repent accordingly. To her utmost sorrow, however, instead of his mind clearing a little, as so often happens after delirium and before death, he gradually fell into a state of coma, and presented every appearance of being actually dead. The doctor was sent for, and the house and grounds were speedily filled with a crowd of people, friends, tenants, fosterers, and poor relatives; one and all anxious to learn the exact condition of the sick man. With tremendous excitement they awaited the exit of the doctor from the house, and, when he at length emerged, they clustered round him and listened for his verdict.

"It's all over, James," he said to the man who was holding his steed, and with those few brief words he climbed into his saddle and rode away. Then the women who were standing by gave a shrill cry, which developed into a continuous, plaintive and discordant groaning, interrupted every now and again by the deep sobbing and groaning, and clapping of hands of Charles' foster-brother, who was moving in and out the crowd, distracted with grief.

All the time Mrs MacCarthy was sitting by the body of her son, the tears streaming from her eyes. Presently some women entered the room and inquired about directions for the ceremony of waking, and providing the refreshments necessary for the occasion. Mournfully the widow gives them the instructions they need, and then continues her solitary vigil, crying with all her soul, and yet quite unaware of the tears that kept pouring from her eyes. So, on and on, with brief intervals only, all through the loud and boisterous lamentations of the visitors over her beloved one, far into the stillness of the night. In one of the interludes, in which she has removed into an inner room to pray, she suddenly hears a low murmuring, which is speedily succeeded by a wild cry of horror, and then, out from the room in which the deceased lies, pour, like some panic-stricken sheep, the entire crowd of those that have participated in the Wake. Nothing daunted, Mrs MacCarthy rushes into the apartment they have quitted, and sees, sitting up on the bed, the light from the candles casting a most unearthly glare on his features, the body of her son. Falling on her knees before it and clasping her hands she at once commences praying; but hearing the word "mother," she springs forward, and, clutching the figure by the arm, shrieks out:

"Speak, in the name of God and His Saints, speak! Are you alive?"

The pale lips move, and finally exclaim:

"Yes, my mother, alive, but sit down and collect yourself."

And then, to the startled and bewildered mother he, whom she had been mourning all this time as dead, unfolded the following remarkable tale.

He declared he remembered nothing of the preliminary stages of his illness, all of which was a blank, and was only cognisant of what was happening when he found himself in another world, standing in the presence of his Creator, Who had summoned him for judgment.

"The dreadful pomp of offended omnipotence," he dramatically stated, "was printed on his brain in characters indelible." What would have happened he dreaded to think, had it not been for his guardian saint, that holy spirit his mother had always taught him to pray to, who was standing by his side, and who pleaded with Him "that one year and one month might be given him on the earth again, in which he should have the opportunity of doing penance and atonement."

After a terribly anxious wait, in which his whole fate—his fate for eternity—hung in the balance, the progress of his kindly intercessor succeeded, and the Great and Awful Judge pronounced these words:

"Return to that world in which thou hast lived but to outrage the laws of Him Who made that world and thee. Three years are given thee for repentance; when these are ended thou shalt again stand here, to be saved or lost for ever."

Charles saw and heard no more; everything became a void, until he suddenly became once again conscious of light and found himself lying on the bed.

He told this experience as if it were no dream, but, as he really believed it to be, an actual reality, and, on his gradually regaining health and strength, he showed the effect it had had on him by completely changing his mode of life. Though not altogether shunning his former companions in folly, he never went to any excess with them, but, on the contrary, often exercised a restraining influence over them, and so, by degrees, came to be looked upon as a person of eminent prudence and wisdom.

The years passed by till at last the third anniversary of the wonderful recovery drew near. As Charles still adhered to his belief that what he had experienced had been no mere dream or wandering of the mind, but an actual visit to spirit land, so nervous did his mother become, as the time drew near for the expiration of the lease of life he declared had been allotted to him, that she wrote to Mrs Barry, a friend of hers, begging her to come with her two girls and stay with her for a few days, until, in fact, the actual day of the third anniversary should have passed.

Unfortunately, Mrs Barry, instead of getting to Spring House, where Mrs Mac-

Carthy lived, on the Wednesday, the day specified in the invitation, was not able to commence the journey till the following Friday, and she then had to leave her eldest daughter behind and bring only the younger one.

What ultimately happened is very graphically described in a letter from the younger girl to the elder. In brief it was this: She and her mother set out in a jaunting-car driven by their man Leary. The recent rains made the road so heavy that they found it impossible to make other than very slow progress, and had to put up for the first night at the house of a Mr Bourke, a friend of theirs, who kept them until late the following day. Indeed, it was evening when they left his premises, with a good fifteen miles to cover before they arrived at Spring House.

The weather was variable, at times the moon shone clear and bright, whilst at others it was covered with thick, black, fast-scudding clouds. The farther they progressed, the more ominous did the elements become, the clouds collected in vast masses, the wind grew stronger and stronger, and presently the rain began to fall. Slow as their progress had been before, it now became slower; at every step the wheels of their car either plunged into a deep slough, or sank almost up to the axle in thick mud.

At last, so impossible did it become, that Mrs Barry inquired of Leary how far they were from Mr Bourke's, the house they had recently left.

"'Tis about ten spades from this to the cross," was the reply, "and we have then only to turn to the left into the avenue, ma'am."

"Very well, then," answered Mrs Barry, "turn up to Mr Bourke's as soon as you reach the crossroads."

Mrs Barry had scarcely uttered these words when a shriek, that thrilled the hearers to the very core of their hearts, burst from the hedge to their right.

It resembled the cry of a female—if it resembled anything earthly at all—struck by a sudden and mortal blow, and giving out life in one long, deep pang of agony.

"Heaven defend us!" exclaimed Mrs Barry. "Go you over the hedge, Leary, and save that woman, if she is not yet dead."

"Woman!" said Leary, beating the horse violently, while his voice trembled. "That's no woman; the sooner we get on, ma'am, the better," and he urged the horse forward.

There was now a heavy spell of darkness as the moon was once again hidden by the clouds, but, though they could see nothing, they heard screams of despair and anguish, accompanied by a loud clapping of the hands, just as if some person on the other side of the hedge was running along in a line with their horse's head, and keeping pace with them.

When they came to within ten yards of the spot where the avenue branched off to Mr Bourke's on the left, and the road to Spring House led away to the right, the moon suddenly reappeared, and they saw, with startling distinctness, the figure of a tall, thin woman, with uncovered head, and long hair floating round her shoulders, attired in a kind of cloak or sheet, standing at the corner of the hedge, just where the road along which they were driving met that which led to Spring House. She had her face turned towards them, and, whilst pointing with her left hand in the direction of Spring House, with her right was beckoning them to hurry. As they advanced she became more and more agitated, until finally, leaping into the road in front of them, and still pointing with outstretched arm in the direction of Spring House, she took up her stand at the entrance to the Avenue, as if to bar their way, and glared defiantly at them.

"Go on, Leary, in God's name!" exclaimed Mrs Barry.

"'Tis the Banshee," said Leary, "and I could not, for what my life is worth, go anywhere this blessed night but to Spring House. But I'm afraid there's something bad going forward, or she would not send us there."

He pressed on towards Spring House, and almost directly afterwards clouds covered the moon, and the Banshee disappeared; the sound of her clapping, though continuing for some time, gradually becoming fainter and fainter, until it finally ceased altogether.

On their arrival at Spring House they learnt that a dreadful tragedy had just taken place.

A lady, Miss Jane Osborn, who was Charles MacCarthy's ward, was to have been married to one James Ryan, and on the day preceding the marriage, as Ryan and Charles MacCarthy were walking together in the grounds of the latter's house, a strange young woman, hiding in the shrubbery, shot Charles in mistake for Ryan, who, it seems, had seduced and deserted her. The wound, which at first appeared trivial, suddenly developed serious symptoms, and before the sun had gone down on the third anniversary of his memorable experience with the Unknown, Charles MacCarthy was again ushered into the presence of his Maker, there to render of himself a second and a final account.

CHAPTER XII

THE BANSHEE IN SCOTLAND

There is, I believe, one version of a famous Scottish haunting in which there figures a Banshee of the more or less orthodox order. I heard it many years ago, and it was told me in good faith, but I cannot, of course, vouch for its authenticity. Since, however, it introduces the Banshee, and, therefore, may be of interest to the readers of this book, I publish it now for the first time, embodied in the following narrative:

"Well, Ronan, you will be glad to hear that I consent to your marrying Ione, provided you can assure me there is nothing wrong with your family history. No hereditary tendencies to drink, disease, or madness. You know I am a great believer in heredity. Your prospects seem good—all the inquiries I have made as to your character have proved satisfactory, and I shall put no obstacles in your way if you can satisfy me on this point. Can you?"

The speaker was Captain Horatio Wynne Pettigrew, R.N., late in command of His Majesty's Frigate *Prometheus*, and now living on retired pay in the small but aristocratic suburb of Birkenhead; the young man he addressed—Ronan Malachy, chief clerk and prospective junior partner in the big business firm of Lowndes, Half & Company, Dublin; and the subject of their conversation—Ione, youngest daughter of the said captain, generally and, perhaps, justly designated the bonniest damsel in all the land between the Dee and the far distant Tweed.

The look of intense suspense and anxiety which had almost contorted Ronan's face while he was waiting for the Captain's reply, now gave way to an expression of the most marked relief.

"I think I have often told you, sir," he replied, "that I have no recollection of my parents, as they both died when I was a baby; but I have never heard either of them spoken of in any other terms than those of the greatest affection and respect. I have always understood my father was lost at sea on a journey either to or from New York, and that my mother, who had a weak heart, died from the effects of the shock. My grandparents on both sides lived together happily, I believe, and died from natural causes at quite a respectable old age. If there had been any hereditary tendencies of an unpleasant nature such as those you name, or any particular family disease, I feel sure I should have heard of it from one or other of my relatives, but I can assure you I have not."

"Very well then," Captain Pettigrew remarked genially, "if your uncle, who is, I understand, your guardian, and whom I know well by reputation, will do me the courtesy to corroborate what you say, I will at once sanction your engagement. But now I must ask you to excuse me, as I have promised to have supper with General Maitland to-night, and before I go have several matters to attend to."

He held out his hand as he spoke, and Ronan, who had been secretly hoping that he would be asked to spend the evening, was reluctantly compelled to withdraw. Outside in the hall, Ione, of course, was waiting, almost beside herself with anxiety, to hear the result of the interview, but Ronan had only time to whisper that it was quite all right, and that her father had been far more amenable than either of them had supposed, before the door of the room he had just left opened, and the Captain appeared.

There was no help for it then, he was obliged to say good-bye, and, having done so, he hurried out into the night.

At the time of which I am writing there were neither motors nor trains, so that Ronan, who, owing to an accident to his horse, had to walk, did not reach home, a distance of some four or five miles, till the evening was well advanced.

On his arrival, burning with impatience to settle the momentous question, he at once broached the subject of his interview with Captain Pettigrew to his uncle, remarking that his fate now rested with him.

"With me!" Mr Malachy exclaimed, placing his paper on an empty chair beside him, and staring at Ronan with a look of sudden bewilderment in his big, short-sighted but extremely benevolent eyes. "Why, you know, my boy, that you have my hearty approval. From all you tell me, Miss Ione must be a very charming young lady; she has aristocratic connections, and will not, I take it, be altogether penniless. Yes, certainly, you have my approval. You have known that all along."

"I have, uncle," Ronan retorted, "and no one is more grateful to you than I. But Captain Pettigrew has very strong ideas about heredity. He believes the tendency to drink, insanity, and sexual lust haunts families, and that, even if it lies dormant for one generation, it is almost bound to manifest itself in another. I told him I was quite sure I was all right in this respect, but he says he wants your corroboration, and that if you will affirm it by letter, he will at once give his consent to my engagement to Ione. I know letter-writing is a confounded nuisance to you, uncle, but do please assure Captain Pettigrew at once that we have no family predisposition of the kind he fears."

Mr Malachy leaned back in his chair and gazed into the long gilt mirror over the mantel-shelf. "Drink and gambling," he said.

"And suicide," Ronan added. "You can at any rate swear to the absence of that in our family — —" but, happening to glance at the mirror as he spoke, he caught in it a reflection of his uncle's face, that at once made him turn round.

"Uncle!" he cried. "Tell me! What is it? Why do you look like that?"

Mr Malachy was silent.

"You're hiding something," Ronan exclaimed sharply. "Tell me what it is. Tell me, I say, and for God's sake put an end to my suspense."

"You are right, Ronan," his uncle responded slowly. "I am hiding something, something I ought perhaps to have told you long ago. It's about your father."

"My father!"

"Yes, your father. I have always told you he was lost at sea. Well, so he was, but in circumstances that were undoubtedly mysterious. He was last seen alive on the wharf at Annan, where he was apparently waiting for a boat to take him to the opposite coast. Someone said they saw him suddenly leap in the water, and some days later a body, declared to be his, was picked up in the Solway Firth."

"Then it was suicide," Ronan gasped. "My God, how awful! Was anyone with him at the time?"

"I don't think I need tell you any more."

"Yes, tell me everything," Ronan answered bitterly. "Nothing makes any difference now. Let me hear all, I insist."

In a voice that shook to such an extent that Ronan looked at him in horror, Mr Malachy continued: "Ronan," he said, "remember that I tell you against my will, and that you are forcing me to speak. They did say at the time that there was a woman with your father—a woman who had travelled with him all the way from Lockerbie—that they quarrelled, that he—he——"

"Yes—go on! For God's sake go on."

"Pushed her in the water—in a rage, mind you, in a rage, I say; and then, apparently appalled at what he had done, jumped in, too."

"Were they both drowned then?"

"Yes."

"And no one tried to save them?"

"No one was near enough. The tide was running strong at the time, and they were both carried out to sea. The woman's body was never found; and your father's, when it was recovered several days afterwards, was so disfigured that it could only be identified by the clothes."

"And they were sure it was my father?"

"I am afraid there is little doubt on that score. Your Aunt Bridget, who, being the last of the family to see him alive, was called upon to identify the body, always declared there was a mistake; she identified the clothes, but mentioned that the body was that of a person whom she had never seen before."

"Then there is a slight hope!"

"I hardly think so, but—but go and see her—it is your only hope, and I will defer writing to Captain Pettigrew until your return."

Early next morning Ronan was well on his way to Lockerbie.

In his present state of mind, every inch was a mile, every second an eternity. If his aunt could only furnish him with some absolute proof that it was not his father who had pushed the woman into the water and afterwards jumped in himself, then he might yet marry the object of his devotion, but, if she could not, he swore with a bitter oath that the water that had claimed his parent, should also claim him; and in the very same spot where the unlucky man who had proved his ruin had perished, he would perish too. It was Ione or obliteration. His whole being concentrated on such thoughts as these, he pressed forward, taking neither rest nor refreshments, till he reached Silloth, where he was compelled to wait several hours, until a fisherman could be prevailed upon to take him across the Solway Firth to Annan.

So far luck had favoured him. The weather had kept fine, and, despite the dangerous condition of the roads, which were notoriously full of footpads, and in the most sorry need of repair, he had covered the distance without mishap.

After leaving Annan, however, disaster at once overtook him. The coach had only proceeded some seven or eight miles along the road to Lockerbie, when a serious accident, through the loss of a wheel, was but narrowly escaped, and, as there seemed little chance of getting the necessary repairs executed that night, the driver suggested that his fares should walk back to Annan and put up at the "Red Star and Garter," till he was able to call for them in the morning.

To this all agreed excepting Ronan, who, scorning the proposal to turn back, declared that he would continue his journey to Lockerbie on foot.

"It's a wild, uncanny bit of country you'll have to go through, mon," the driver remonstrated, "and I'm nae sure but what you may come across some of them smuggler laddies from away across the borders of Kirkcudbright. They are fair sore just noo at the way in which the Custom House officials are treating them, and are downright suspicious of everyone they meet. You'll be weel guided to return to the coast with us."

To this well-intentioned advice Ronan did not even condescend a reply, but, bidding his fellow-passengers good night, he buttoned his overcoat tightly round his chest, and stepped resolutely forward into the darkness.

The driver had not exaggerated. It was a wild, uncouth bit of country. The road itself was a mere track, all ruts and furrows, with nothing to denote its boundaries saving ditches, or black tarns that gleamed fitfully whenever the moonbeams, emerging from behind black masses of clouds, fell on them. Beyond the road, on one side, was a wide stretch of barren moorland, terminating at the foot of a long line of rather low and singularly funereal-looking hills; and, on the other, a black, thickly wooded chasm, at the bottom of which thundered a river. In every fitful outburst of lunar splendour each detail in the landscape stood out with almost microscopic clearness, but otherwise all lay heavily shrouded in an almost impenetrable mantle of gloom, from which there seemed to emanate strange, indefinable shadows, that, as far as Ronan could see, had no material counterparts.

Naturally stout of heart and afraid of nothing, Ronan was, at the same time, a Celt, and possessed, in no small degree, all the Celtic awe and respect for anything associated with the supernatural. Hence, though he pushed steadily on and kept picturing to himself the face and form of his lady love, to win whom he was fully prepared to go to any extremity, he could not prevent himself from occasionally glancing with misgiving at some more than usually perplexing shadow, or, from time to time, prevent his heart from beating louder at the rustle of a gorse-bush, or the dismal hooting of an owl. In some mysterious fashion the night seemed to have suddenly changed everything, and to have vested every object and every trifling—or what in the daytime would have been trifling—sound with a significance that was truly enigmatical and startling.

The air, however, with its blending of scents from the pines, and gorse, and heather, with ozone from the not far distant Solway Firth, was so delicious that Ronan kept throwing back his head to inhale great draughts of it; and it was whilst he thus stood a second, with his nostrils and forehead upturned, that he first became aware of an impending storm. At first a few big splashes, and the low moaning of the wind as it swept towards and past him from the far distant hill-tops; then more splashes, and then a downpour.

Ronan, who was now walking abreast a low white wall, beyond which he could see one of those shelters that in Scotland are erected everywhere for the protection of both cattle and sheep from the terrible blizzards that nearly every winter devastate the country, perceiving the futility and danger of trying to face the storm, made for the wall and, climbing it, dropped over on the other side. As bad luck would have it, however, he alighted on a boulder and, unable to retain his foothold, slipped off it, striking his head a severe blow on the ground. For some seconds he lay unconscious, then, his senses gradually returning, he picked himself up and made for the shelter.

Stumbling blindly forward towards the entrance of the building, he collided with a figure that suddenly seemed to rise from the ground, and for a moment his heart stood still, but his fears were quickly dissipated by the unmistakable sound of a human voice.

"Who is that?" someone inquired in tremulous tones. "Oh, sir, are you one of the revellers?"

"One of the revellers?" Ronan replied. "It's an ill night for any revelling. What do you mean?"

"I mean, are you one of the young men going to the fancy dress dance at the Spelkin Towers," the voice responded. "But your accent tells me you are not; you don't belong to these parts. You are Irish."

"That is truly said," Ronan answered. "My home is in Dublin, and it's the first time I have set foot on Dumfries soil, and I'll stake every penny in my purse it will be the last. I'm bound for Lockerbie, but I'm thinking it will be the early hours of the morning before I get there."

"For Lockerbie," the voice replied. "Why that's a distance of about twenty miles. It's a straight road, however, and you pass the Spelkin Towers on the way. It stands in a clump of trees about a hundred yards back from the road, on this side of it, about three miles from here. If there were a moon you would easily recognise the place by the big white gate leading directly to it."

"So I might, but why waste my time and your breath. The Spelkins, or whatever you call it, has naught to do with me. I'm bound for Lockerbie, I tell you, and as the rain seems to be abating I intend moving on again."

"Sir," the woman pleaded, "I pray you stay a few moments and listen to what I have to say. A gentleman is going to the revels to-night for whom I have a letter of the utmost importance. His name is Dunloe—Mr Robert Dunloe of Annan. He is due at the Towers at eight o'clock, and should surely be passing here almost at this very moment. But, sir, I durst not wait for him any longer, as I have an aged mother at home who has been taken suddenly and violently ill. For mercy's sake I beg of you to wait and give him the letter in my stead."

"Give him the letter in your stead!" Ronan ejaculated. "Why, I may never see him—indeed, the odds are a thousand to one I never shall. I'm in a hurry, too. I can't stay hanging around here all night. Besides, how should I know him?"

"He's dressed as a jester," the woman answered, "and if the wind is not blowing too strong you'll hear the sound of his bells. He's sure to be coming by very soon. Oh, sir, do me this favour, I pray you."

As she spoke the rain ceased and the moon, suddenly appearing from behind a bank of clouds, revealed her face. It was startlingly white, and in a strange, elfish kind of way, beautiful. Ronan gazed at it in astonishment, it was altogether so different from the face he had pictured from the voice, and as he stared down into the big, black eyes raised pleadingly to his, he felt curiously fascinated, and all idea of resistance at once departed.

"All right," he said slowly, "I will do as you wish. A man in Court-jester's costume, with jingling bells, answering to the name of Robert Dunloe. Hand me the letter, and I will wait in the road till he passes."

She obeyed, and, taking from her bosom an envelope, handed it to him.

"Oh, sir," she said softly, "I can't tell you how grateful I am. It is most kind of you—most chivalrous, and I am sure you will one day be rewarded. Hark! footsteps. A number of them. It must be some of the revellers. I must remain here till they pass, for I would not for the world have them see me; they are rude, boisterous fellows, and have little respect for a maiden when they meet her alone on the highway. There have been some dreadful doings of late around here."

She laid one of her little white hands on Ronan's arm as she spoke, and, with the forefinger of the other placed on her lips, enjoined silence. Then as the footsteps and voices, which had been drawing nearer and nearer, passed close to them and died gradually away in the distance, she hurriedly bade Ronan farewell, and darted nimbly away in the darkness.

Ronan stood for some minutes where she had left him, half expecting she would reappear, but at last, convinced that she had really taken her departure, he climbed the wall, back again into the road, and waited. Had it not been for the envelope, which certainly felt material enough, Ronan would have been inclined to attribute it all to some curious kind of hallucination—the girl was so different—albeit so subtly and inexplicably different—from anyone he had ever seen before. But that envelope with the name "Robert Dunloe, Esquire," so clearly and beautifully superscribed on it, was a proof of her reality, and, as he stood fingering the missive and pondering the subject over in his mind, he once again heard the sound of footsteps. This time they were the footsteps of one person only, and, as he had been led to expect, they were accompanied by the faint jingle, jingle of bells.

The moon, now quite free from clouds, rendered every object so clearly visible that Ronan, looking in the direction from which the sounds came, soon detected a tall, oddly attired figure, whilst still a long way off, advancing towards him with big, swinging strides. Had he not been prepared for someone in fancy costume, Ronan might have felt somewhat alarmed, for a Scotch moor in the dead of winter is hardly the place where one would expect to encounter a masquerader in jester's costume.

Moreover, though the magnifying action of the moon's rays were probably accountable for it, there seemed to be something singularly bizarre about the figure, apart from its clothes; its head seemed abnormally round and small, its limbs abnormally long and emaciated, and its movements remarkably automatic and at the same time spiderlike.

Ronan gripped the envelope in his hand—it was solid enough; therefore, the queer, fantastic-looking thing, stalking so grotesquely towards him, must be solid too—a mere man—and Ronan forced a laugh. Another moment, and he had stepped out from under cover of the wall.

"Are you Mr Robert Dunloe?" he asked, "because, if so, I have a letter for you."

The figure halted, and the white, parchment-like face with two very light green, cat-like eyes, bent down and favoured Ronan with a half-frightened, but penetrating gaze.

"Yes," came the reply, "I am Mr Dunloe. But how came you with a letter for me? Give it to me at once." And before Ronan could prevent him, he had snatched the envelope from his grasp, and, having broken open the seal, was reading the contents.

"Ah!" he ejaculated. "What a fool! I might have known so all along, but it's not too late." Then he folded the letter in his hand and stood holding it, apparently buried in thought.

Ronan, whose hot Irish temper had been roused by the rude manner in which the stranger had obtained possession of the missive, would have moved on and left him, had he not felt restrained by the same peculiar fascination he had experienced when talking to the girl.

"I trust," he at length remarked, "that your letter contains no ill news. The lady who requested me to give it you mentioned the fact that a relative of hers had been taken very ill."

"When and where did you see her?" the stranger queried, his eyes once again seeking Ronan's face with the same fixed, penetrating stare.

"In that shelter over there," Ronan answered, pointing to it. "We were strangers to one another, and I was sheltering from the storm. I explained to her that I was on my way to Lockerbie, and in no little hurry to get there, but she begged me so earnestly to await your arrival, so that I might hand you the letter, that she might be free to return home at once, that I consented. That is all that passed between us."

"She went?"

"Yes, she slipped away suddenly in the darkness, where I don't know."

The stranger mused for a few moments, stroking his chin with long, lean fingers. Then he suddenly seemed to wake up, and spoke again, but this time in a far more courteous fashion.

"Young man," he said, "I believe you. You have a candid expression in your eyes, and an honest ring in your voice. Men that speak in such tones seldom lie. You are kind-hearted, too, and I am going to ask of you a favour. Yesterday morning, in Annan, two of the leading townsfolk laid me a wager that I would not attend a ball to-night at the Spelkin Towers, and, attired as a Court jester, walk all the way to and fro, no matter how inclement the weather. I accepted the challenge, and now, having progressed so far, I should aim at completing my task, but for this letter, which fully corroborates what the young lady told you, and informs me that a very old and dear friend of mine is dying, and would at all costs see me at once, as she has an important statement to make for my ears only. Now, sir, I cannot possibly go to her in these outlandish clothes, lest the shock of seeing me so attired should prove too much for her in her present serious condition. Can I prevail upon your charity and chivalry—for once again it is on behalf of a woman—and good Christian spirit—for I doubt not, from your demeanour, that you have been brought up in a truly God-fearing and pious manner—to persuade you to change costumes with me over yonder in that shed. I would then be able to appear before my poor, dying friend in suitable, sober garments, whilst you would be free to go to the ball, and, by posing as Mr Robert Dunloe, share the proceeds of my wager with me."

Then, noting the expression that came over Ronan's face, he added quickly:

"You will incur no risks. I am a comparative stranger in these parts—none of the revellers know me by sight. All you will have to do on your arrival at the Towers will be to explain to your host, Sir Hector McBlane, the nature of the wager, and ask him to give you some record of your attendance that I can subsequently show to my two friends. Remember, sir, that it is not only for the sake of gratifying a dying woman's wish that I am asking this favour of you, but it is also to make sure that the young lady who gave you the letter shall not be jeopardised."

Ronan hesitated. Had such a mystifying proposition been made to him on any other occasion he would, perhaps, have rejected it at once as the sheerest lunacy; but there was something about this night—the wild grandeur of the silent moonlit scenery, the intoxicating sweetness of the subtly scented air, to say nothing of the maiden whose elfish appearance had seemed in such absolute harmony both with the soft, silvery starlight and the black granite boulders—that was wholly different from anything Ronan had ever experienced before, and his deeply emotional and easily excited temperament, rising in hot rebellion against his reason, urged him to embark upon what he persuaded himself might prove a vastly entertaining adventure. He consequently agreed to do as the stranger suggested, and, accompanying him into the shelter, he exchanged clothes with him.

After arranging to meet in the same spot at four o'clock in the morning, the two men parted, the stranger making off across the moors, and Ronan continuing along the high road.

Nothing of moment occurred again till Ronan caught sight of the clump of pines, from the centre of which rose the Spelkin Towers, and a few yards farther on perceived the white wooden gate that the elfish maiden had described to him. On his approach, several figures, in fancy dress and wearing dominoes, advanced to meet him, and one, with a low bow, inquired if he had the honour of addressing Mr Robert Dunloe.

"Why, yes," Ronan responded, with some astonishment, "but I did not think anyone knew I was coming here to-night saving our host, Sir Hector McBlane."

"That is because you are so modest," was the reply. "I can assure you, Mr Dunloe, your fame has preceded you, and everyone present here to-night will be eagerly looking forward to the moment of your arrival. Let me introduce you to my friends. Sir Frederick Clanstradie, Sir Austin Maltravers, Lord Henry Baxter, Mr Leslie de Vaux."

Each of the guests bowed in turn as their names were pronounced, and then, at a signal from the spokesman, who informed Ronan he was Sir Philip McBlane, cousin to their host, they proceeded in a body to the queerly constructed mansion.

Inside Ronan could see no sign whatever of any festivity, but on being told that Sir Hector was awaiting him in the ball-room, he allowed himself to be conducted along a bare, gloomy passage and down a narrow flight of steep stone steps into a large dungeon-like chamber, piled up in places with strange-looking lumber, and in one corner of which he perceived a tall figure, draped from head to foot in the hideous black garments of a Spanish inquisitor, standing in the immediate vicinity of a heap of loose bricks and freshly made mortar, and bending over a cauldron full of what looked like simmering tar. The whole aspect of the room was indeed so grim and forbidding, that Ronan drew back in dismay and turned to Sir Philip and his comrades for an explanation.

Before, however, anyone could speak, the figure in the inquisitorial robes advanced, and, bidding Ronan welcome, declared that he considered it both an honour and a privilege to entertain so illustrious a guest.

Not knowing how to reply to a greeting that seemed so absurdly exaggerated, Ronan merely mumbled out something to the effect that he was delighted to come, and then lapsed into an awkward and embarrassed silence, during which he could feel the eyes of everyone fixed on him with an expression he could not for the life of him make out.

Finally, the inquisitor, whom Ronan now divined was Sir Hector McBlane, after expressing a hope that the ladies would soon make their appearance, invited the gentlemen to partake of some refreshments.

Bottles scattered in untidy profusion upon a plain deal table were then un-corked, and the sinisterly clad host proposed they should all drink a toast of wel-come to their distinguished guest, Mr Robert Dunloe.

Up to the present Ronan had only been conscious of what seemed to him courtesy and cordiality in the voices of his fellow-guests, but now, as one and all clinked glasses and shouted in unison, "For he's a jolly good fellow, and so say all of us," he fancied he could detect something rather different; what it was he could not say, but it gave him the same feeling of doubt and uncertainty as had the ex-pression in their faces immediately after his introduction to Sir Hector.

Again there was an embarrassed silence, which was eventually broken by Ronan, who, perceiving that something was expected from him, at length stood up and responded to the toast.

His speech was of very short duration, but it was hardly over, before a loud rapping of high-heeled shoes sounded on the stone steps, and a number of wom-en, dressed in every conceivable fashion, from the quaintly picturesque costume of the Middle Ages to the still fondly remembered and popular Empire gown, came trooping into the room. Their curiously clumsy movements caused Ronan to scru-tinise them somewhat closely, but it was not until, in response to a wild outburst on wheezy flutes and derelict bagpipes, the assembly commenced dancing, that he awoke to the fact which now seemed obvious enough, that these weird-looking women were not women at all, but merely men mummers.

For the next few minutes the noise and confusion were such that Ronan, whose temples had been set on fire by the wine, hardly knew whether he was standing on his head or his feet. First one of the pretended women, and then another, solicited the honour of dancing with him, until at last, through sheer fatigue and giddiness, he was constrained to stop and lean for support against the walls of the building.

He was still in this attitude, when the music, if such one could style it, sudden-ly ceased, and the whole company, as if by a preconcerted signal, suddenly stood at attention, as still and silent as statues.

Sir Hector McBlane then approached Ronan with a bow, and informing him that his bride awaited him in the bridal chamber, declared that the time had now arrived for his introduction to her.

This announcement was so unexpected and extraordinary that Ronan lost all power of speech, and, before he could realise what was taking place, he found himself being conducted by his host to a dimly lighted corner of the room, where he perceived, for the first time, a recess or kind of cell, measuring not more than four feet in depth, and three feet across, but reaching upwards to the same height as the ceiling. Exactly in the centre of it was a tall figure, absolutely stiff and mo-tionless, and clad in long, flowing, white garments.

Still too bewildered and astonished to protest or remonstrate, Ronan permit-ted himself to be led right up to the figure, which a sudden flare from a torch held by one of the revellers, enabled him to perceive was merely a huge rag doll, decked out in sham jewellery, with a painted, leering face and a mass of tow hair, a clever but ridiculous caricature of a woman. He was about to demand an angry explanation of the foolery, when he was pushed violently forward, and, before he could recover his equilibrium, a rope was wound several times round his body, and he was strapped tightly to the doll, which was securely attached to an iron stake fixed perpendicularly in the ground.

Loud shouts of laughter now echoed from one end of the chamber to the other, the merriment being further increased when Sir Hector, with an assumed gravity, presented his humblest respects to the bride and bridegroom, and hoped that they would enjoy a long and very happy honeymoon.

Ronan, whose indignation was by this time raised to boiling pitch, furiously demanded to be released, but the more angry he became, the more his tormentors mocked, until at length even walls, floor, and ceiling seemed to become infected and to shake with an uncontrollable and devilish mirth. Finally, however, when things had gone on in this fashion for some time, Sir Hector again spoke, and this time announced in loud tones that, as he was quite sure the bride and bridegroom must now be wishing for nothing better than to be left to themselves, he and his guests would now proceed to seal up the bridal chamber.

A general bustle and subsequent clinking of metal on the stone floor, immediately following this speech, left Ronan in no doubt whatever as to what was happening. He was, of course, being bricked up. Now although he felt assured that it was all a joke, he also felt it was a joke that had gone on quite long enough. It was only too clear to him that, for some reason or another, Mr Robert Dunloe was very far from popular with these masqueraders, and he began to wonder if Mr Dunloe's explanation of his desire to exchange clothes was the correct one, whether, in fact, Mr Dunloe had not got an inkling of what was going to happen to him from the elfish girl's letter, and whether he had not merely trumped up the story of the sick woman and the wager for the occasion.

In any case Ronan felt that he had been let down badly, and since he did not see why he should still pretend to be the man who had taken such advantage of him, he called out:

"Look here, I've a confession to make. You think I'm Mr Robert Dunloe, but I'm not. My name is Ronan Malachy. I'm staying with my uncle, Mr Hugh Malachy, near Birkenhead, and anyone there would confirm my identity. I was bound to-night for Lockerbie, when I met a girl who begged me to wait in the road and deliver a letter for her to an individual dressed as a Court jester, and styling himself Robert Dunloe, who would presently pass by. Not liking to refuse a lady, I agreed, and when I had given the man the letter, and he had read it, he told me that it was a summons to attend the death-bed of a very dear friend and urged me to exchange clothes with him, in order that he might go suitably attired. To this I naturally assented, and he then begged me to impersonate him here, as he had laid a big wager that he would be present at this ball and would walk all the way from Annan in this costume."

Ronan was about to add more, when Sir Hector McBlane approached the mound of bricks, which was already breast high, and, looking straight at him, exclaimed:

"Robert Dunloe, it is useless to try and hoodwink us. We know all about you. We know that you were once arrested for highway robbery and murder, but got off through turning King's evidence against your mate, 'Hal of the seventeen strings,' who was hanged at Lancaster; that you then, took up Government spying as a trade, and got a score of the best fellows who ever breathed life sentences at Morecombe for smuggling a few casks of brandy. A month ago we heard that you were coming to Annan to try and place a rope round some of our necks for the same so-called felony, and we determined that we would be first in the field and teach you a lesson. We are now going to seal you up and leave you to soliloquise over the rope which is round you, and which is, doubtless, of the same hue and texture as that which has hanged the many that have been sentenced through your treachery. Adieu."

It was in vain, when Sir Hector had finished speaking, that Ronan alternately pleaded and swore; he could get no further reply. The layers of bricks rose, till only one was left to render the task complete; and already the air within was becoming fetid and oppressive. A terrible sense of utter and hopeless isolation now surged through Ronan, and forced him once again to call out:

"For the love of God," he said, "set me free. For the LOVE OF GOD."

He had barely uttered these words, when the whole assembly looked at one another with startled faces.

"Hark!" exclaimed one. "Do you hear that screaming and clapping? What in the world is it?"

"I should say," said another, "that it was some puir bairn being done to death were it not for the clapping, but that gets over me. Whatever can it mean?"

At that moment steps were heard descending the stairs in a great hurry, and a young man, with bright red hair, and dressed strictly in accordance with the fashion prevailing at that time, burst into the room.

"Boys," he exclaimed, his voice shaking with emotion, "I have just seen the Banshee. She was in the road outside the gates of this house, running backwards and forwards, just as I saw her five years ago in Kerry, and, as I tried to pass her by to get on my way to Dumfries, she waved me back, shaking her fist and screaming at the same time. Then she signalled to me to come here, and ran on ahead of me, crying, and groaning, and clapping her hands. And as I knew it would be as much as my life is worth to disobey her, I followed. You can still hear her outside, keening and screeching. But what are all these bricks for, and this mortar?"

"The informer, Robert Dunloe," exclaimed one of the revellers. "We have been bricking him up for a lark, and intend keeping him here till the morning."

"It's a lie," Ronan shouted. "I'm no more Dunloe than any of you. I'm Ronan Malachy, I tell you, and my home is in Dublin. I heard an Irish voice just now, surely he can tell I'm Irish, too."

"Arrah, I believe you," said the new-comer. "It's the real brogue you've got, and none other, though it's not so pronounced as is my own; but may be you've lived longer in this country than I. Pull down those bricks, boys, and let me have a look at him."

"No, no," cried several voices, angrily. "Anybody could take you in, Pat. He's Dunloe right enough; and now we've got him, we intend to keep him."

In the altercation that now ensued, some sided with the Irishman, and some against him; but over and above all the clamour and confusion the voice of the Banshee could still be heard shrieking, and wailing, and clapping her hands.

At last someone struck a blow, and in an instant swords were drawn, sticks and cudgels were used, furniture was flung about freely, and table, brazier, and cauldron were overturned; and the blazing pitch and red hot coals, coming in contact with piled up articles of all kinds—casks, chests, boxes, musty old books, paper and logs—it was not long before the whole chamber became a mass of flames.

One or two of the calmer and more sober revellers attempted to get to the recess and batter down the bricks, which were merely placed together without cement, but the fury of the flames drove them back, and the hapless Ronan was, in the end, abandoned to his fate.

Hideously aware of what was going on, he struggled desperately to free himself, and, at last succeeding, made a frantic attempt to reach a small window, placed at a height of some seven or eight feet from the floor. After several fruitless efforts he triumphed, only to discover, however, that the aperture was just too small for his body to pass through.

The flames had, by this time, reached the entrance to the recess, and the heat from them was so stupendous that Ronan, weak and exhausted after his long fast and all the harrowing and exciting moments he had passed through, let go his hold, and, falling backwards, struck his head a terrific crash on the floor.

Much to his amazement, on recovering his faculties, Ronan found himself lying out of doors. Above him was no abysmal darkness, only the heavens brilliantly lighted by moon and stars, whilst as far as his sight could travel was free and open space, a countryside dotted here and there with gorse bushes and the silvery shimmering surface of moorland tarns. He turned round, and close beside him was a big boulder of rock that he now remembered slipping from when he had dropped over the wall to take cover from the storm. And there, sure enough, was the shelter. He got up and went towards it. It was quite deserted, no one was there, not even a cow, and the silence that came to him was just the ordinary silence of the night, with nothing in it weirder or more arrestive than the rushing of distant water and the occasional croaking of a toad. Considerably mystified, and unable to decide in his mind whether all he had gone through had been a dream or not, he now clambered back into the road and pursued his way, according to his original intention, towards Lockerbie.

On reaching the spot where he had in his dream, or whatever it was, first sighted the Spelkin Towers, he perceived, to his amazement, the very same building, apparently exact in every detail. On approaching nearer he found the white gate, but whereas when he had beheld the Towers only such a short time ago, there had been a feeble flicker of artificial light in some of the slit-like windows, all was now gloomy and deserted, and, still further to his amazement, he perceived, on opening the gate and entering, that the building was, to some extent, in ruins, and that the charred timber and blackened walls gave every indication of its having been partially destroyed by fire.

Totally unable to account for his experience, but convinced in his own mind that it was not all a dream, he now hurried on, and reached his aunt's house in Lockerbie, just in time to wash and tidy himself for breakfast.

After the meal, and when he was sitting with his aunt by the fire in the drawing-room, Ronan not only announced to her the purpose of his visit, but gave her a detailed account of his journey and adventures on the way, asking her in conclusion what she thought of his experience, whether she believed it to be merely a dream or, in very truth, an encounter with the denizens of ghostland.

Miss Bridget Malachy, who during Ronan's recitation obviously had found it extremely difficult to maintain silence, now gave vent to her feelings.

"I cannot tell you," she said excitedly, "how immensely interested I am in all you have told me. Last night was the anniversary of your father's strange disappearance. I had only been living here a few weeks, when I received a letter from him, saying he had business to transact in the North of England, and would like to spend two or three days with me. He gave me the exact route he intended to travel by from Dublin, and the exact hour he expected to arrive. Your father was the most precise man I ever met.

"Well, on the night before the day he was due to arrive, as I was sitting in this very room, writing, I suddenly heard a tapping at the window, as if produced by the beak and claws of some bird, or very long finger nails. Wondering what it could be, I got up, and, pulling aside the blind, received the most violent shock. There, looking directly in at me, with an expression of the most intense sorrow and pity in its eyes, was the face of a woman. The cheeks shone with a strange, startling whiteness, and the long, straggling hair fell in a disordered mass low over her neck and shoulders. As her gaze met mine she tapped the window with her long, white fingers and, throwing back her head, uttered the most harrowing, heart-rending scream. Convinced now that she was the Banshee, which I had often had described to me by my friends, I was not so much frightened as interested, and I was about to address her and ask her what in God's name she wanted, when she abruptly vanished, and I found myself staring into space.

"A week later, I received tidings that a body, believed to be your father's, had just been recovered from the Solway Firth, and I was asked to go at once and identify it. I went, and though it had remained in the water too long, perhaps, to be easily recognisable, I was absolutely certain my surmises were correct, and that the body was that of a stranger. It was that of a man somewhat taller than your father, and the tips of his fingers, moreover, were spatulate, whereas, like all the rest of our family's, your father's fingers were pointed. From what you have told me I am now convinced that I really was right, and that your father, falling into the hands of the smugglers, who, at that time, infested the whole of this neighbourhood, did actually meet with foul play. I recollect perfectly well the fire at the Spelkin Towers the night your father disappeared, but, until now, I never in any way associated the event with him. Do, I beseech you, make a thorough search of the ruins and see if you can find anything that will help to substantiate your story and prove that your experience was of a nature very different from that of an ordinary dream."

Ronan needed no further bidding. Accompanied by his aunt's gardener and two or three villagers—for the gardener would not venture there without a formidable escort; the place, he said, bore a most evil and sinister reputation—he at once proceeded to the Towers, and, in one of the cellars, bricked up in a recess, they found a skeleton—the skeleton of a man, on one of whose fingers was a signet-ring, which Miss Bridget Malachy at once identified as having belonged to her missing brother. Moreover, with the remains were a few tattered shreds—all that was left of the clothes—and, though blackened and rusty, a number of tiny bells, such as might have once adorned the cap of a Court jester.

The Spelkin Towers is still haunted, for it has ghosts of its own, but never, I believe, since that memorable experience of Ronan's within its grey and lichen-covered walls, has it again been visited by the Banshee.

CHAPTER XIII
MY OWN EXPERIENCES WITH THE BANSHEE

In order definitely to establish my claim to the Banshee, I am obliged to state here that the family to which I belong is the oldest branch of the O'Donnells, and dates back in direct unbroken line to Niall of the Nine Hostages. I am therefore genuinely Celtic Irish, but, in addition to that, I have in my veins strains both of the blood of the O'Briens of Thomond (whose Banshee visited Lady Fanshawe), and of the O'Rourkes, Princes of Brefni; for my ancestor, Edmund O'Donnell, married Bridget, daughter of O'Rourk of the house of Brefni, and his mother was the daughter of Donat O'Brien of the house of Thomond. All of which, and more, may be ascertained by a reference to the Records of the Truagh O'Donnells.[15]

Possibly my first experience of the Banshee occurred before I was old enough to take note of it. I lost my father when I was a baby. He left home with the intention of going on a brief visit to Palestine, but, meeting on the way an ex-officer of the Anglo-Indian army, who had been engaged by the King of Abyssinia to help in the work of remodelling the Abyssinian army, he abandoned his idea of visiting the Holy Land, and decided to go to Abyssinia instead.

What actually happened then will probably never be known. His death was reported to have taken place at Arkiko, a small village some two hours walking distance from Massowah, and from the letters[16] subsequently received from the French Consul at Massowah and several other people, as well as from the entries in his diary (the latter being recovered with other of his personal effects and sent home with them), there seems to have been little, if any, doubt that he was trapped and murdered, the object being robbery.

The case created quite a sensation at the time, and is referred to in a work entitled "The Oriental Zig-zag," by Charles Hamilton, who, I believe, stayed some few years later at the house at Massowah, where my father lodged, and was stated to have shared his fate.

With regard to the supernatural happenings in connection with the event. The house that my father had occupied before setting out for the East was semi-detached, the first house in a row, which at that time was not completed. It was situ-

---

[15] See Records of the Truagh O'Donnells in the Office of the King of Arms, Dublin. Refs.: Genealogias, Vol. XI., p. 327; Register XV., p. 5; Register XXII., p. 286; and Sheridan, p. 323.

[16] The originals are still in existence. The diary was kept right up to the night preceding his death.

ated in a distinctly lonely spot. On the one side of it, and to the rear, were gardens, bounded by fields, and people rarely visited the place after nightfall.

On the night preceding my father's death, my mother was sitting in the din-ing-room, which overlooked the back garden, reading. It was a windy but fine night, and, save for the rustling of the leaves, and an occasional creaking of the shutters, absolutely still. Suddenly, from apparently just under the window, there rang out a series of the most harrowing screams. Immeasurably startled, and fear-ing, at first, that it was some woman being murdered in the garden, my mother summoned the servants, and they all listened. The sounds went on, every moment increasing in vehemence, and there was an intensity and eeriness about them that speedily convinced the hearers that they could be due to no earthly agency. After lasting several minutes they finally died away in a long, protracted wail, full of such agony and despair, that my mother and her companions were distressed beyond words.

As soon as they could summon up the courage they went out and scoured the gardens, but though they looked everywhere, and there was little cover for anyone to hide, they could discover nothing that could in any way account for the noises. A dreadful fear then seized my mother. She believed that she had heard the Banshee which my father had often spoken about to her, and she was little sur-prised, when, in a few days time, the news reached her that my father was dead. He had died about dawn, the day after my mother and the servants had heard the screaming. I sent an account of the incident, together with other phenomena that happened about the same time, signed by two of the people who experienced them, to the Society for Psychical Research, who published it in their journal in the autumn of 1899.

I have vivid recollections of my mother telling me about it when I was a little boy, and I remember that every time I heard the shutters in the room where we sat rattle, and the wind moan and sigh in the chimney, I fully expected to hear terrible shrieks ring out, and to see some white and ghastly face pressed against the win-dow-panes, peering in at me. After these recitations I was terrified at the darkness, and endured, when alone in my bedroom, agonies of mind that no grown-up per-son, perhaps, could ever realise. The house and garden, so very bright and cheer-ful, and in every way ordinary, in the daytime, when the sun was out, seemed to be entirely metamorphosed directly it was dusk. Shadows assuredly stranger than any other shadows—for as far as I could see they had no material counterpart—used to congregate on the stairs, and darken the paths and lawn.

There were always certain spots that frightened me more than others, a bend in one of the staircases, for example, the banisters on the top landing, a passage in the basement of the house, and the path leading from the gate to the front door. Even in the daytime, occasionally, I was chary about passing these places. I felt by instinct something uncanny was there; something that was grotesque and sin-ister, and which had specially malevolent designs toward me. When I was alone I hurried past, often with my eyes shut; and at night time, I am not ashamed to admit, I often ran. Yet, at that time I had no knowledge that others beside myself thought these things and had these experiences. I did not know, for instance, that once, when my youngest sister, who was a little older than I, was passing along that passage I so much dreaded, she heard, close beside her, a short, sharp laugh, or chuckle, and so expressive of hatred and derision, that the sound of it haunted her memory ever after. I also did not know then that one evening, immediately prior to my father's death, when another of my sisters was running up the stairs, she saw, peering down at her from over the banisters on that top landing I so much dreaded, a face which literally froze her with horror. Crowned with a mass of disordered tow-coloured hair, the skin tightly drawn over the bones like a mummy, it looked as if it had been buried for several months and then resurrected. The light, obliquely set eyes, suffused with baleful glee, stared straight at her, while the mouth, just such a mouth as might have made that chuckle, leered. It did not seem to her to be the face of anyone that had ever lived, but to belong to an entirely different species, and to be the creation of something wholly evil. She looked at it for some seconds, too petrified to move or cry out, until, her faculties gradually reassuring themselves, she turned round from the spot and flew downstairs.

Some years later, just before the death of my mother, at about the same time of day and in precisely the same place, the head was again seen, this time by my younger sister, the one who had heard the ghostly chuckle.

I think, without doubt, that the chuckle, no less than the head, must be attributed to the malignant Banshee. I may add, perhaps, without digressing too much, that supernatural happenings, apart from the Banshee, were associated with both my parents' deaths. On the night following my father's murder, and on every subsequent night for a period of six weeks, my mother and the servants were aroused regularly at twelve o'clock by a sound, as of someone hammering down the lids of packing-cases, issuing from the room in the basement of the house, which my father had always used as a study. They then heard footsteps ascending the stairs and pausing outside each bedroom in turn, which they all recognised as my father's, and, occasionally, my old nurse used to see the door of the night nursery open, and a light, like the light of a candle outside, whilst at the same time she would hear, proceeding from the landing, a quick jabber, jabber, jabber, as of someone talking very fast, and trying very hard to say something intelligible. No one was ever seen when this voice and the footsteps, said to be my father's, were heard, but this circumstance may be accounted for by the fact that my father, just before leaving Ireland, had remarked to my mother that, should anything happen to him abroad, he would in his spirit appear to her; and she, growing pale at the mere thought, begged him to do no such thing, whereupon he had laughingly replied:

"Very well then, I will find some other means of communicating with you."

Many manifestations of a similar nature to the foregoing, and also, like the foregoing, having nothing to do with the Banshee, occurred immediately after the death of my mother, but of these I must give an account on some future occasion.

Years passed, and nothing more was seen or heard of the Banshee till I was grown up. After leaving school I went to Dublin to read with Dr Chetwode Crawley, in Ely Place, for the Royal Irish Constabulary, and I might, I think, have passed into that Force, had it not been for the fact that at the preliminary medical examination some never-to-be-forgotten and, as I thought then, intensely ill-natured doctor, rejected me. Accordingly, I never entered for the literary, but returned home thoroughly dispirited, and faced with the urgent necessity of at once looking around for something to do. However, in a very short time I had practically settled on going to America to a ranch out West (a most disastrous venture as it subsequently proved to be), and it was immediately after I had reached this decision that my first actual experience with what I believe to have been the malevolent family Banshee occurred. It happened in the same house in which the other supernatural occurrences had taken place. All the family, saving myself, were away at the time, and I was the sole occupant of one of the landings, the servants being all together on another floor.

I had gone to bed early, and had been sleeping for some time, when I was awakened about two o'clock by a loud noise, for which I could not account, and which reverberated in my ears for fully half a minute. I was sitting up, still wondering what on earth could have produced it, when, immediately over my head, I heard a laugh, an abrupt kind of chuckle, that was so malicious and evil that I could not possibly attribute it to any human agency, but rather to some entity of wholly satanic origin, and which my instinct told me was one of our attendant Banshees. I got out of bed, struck a light, and made a thorough investigation, not only of the room, but the landing outside. There was no one there, nothing, as far as I could see, that could in any way explain the occurrence. I threw open the bedroom window and looked out. The night was beautiful — the sky brilliantly illuminated with moon and stars — and everything perfectly still, excepting for the very faintest rustling of the leaves as the soft night breeze swept through the branches and set them in motion. I listened for some time, but, the hush continuing, I at last got back again into bed, and eventually fell asleep. I mentioned the incident in the morning to the servants, and they, too, had heard it.

A short time afterwards I went to the United States, and had the most unhappy and calamitous experience in my whole career.

My next experience of the Banshee happened two or three years later, when, having returned from America, I was living in Cornwall, running a small preparatory school, principally for delicate boys.

The house I occupied was quite new, in fact I was the first tenant, and had watched it being built. It was the last house in a terrace, and facing it was a cliff, at the foot of which ran a steep path leading to the beach. At this particular time there was no one in the house but my aged housekeeper, by name Mrs Bolitho, and myself, and whilst Mrs Bolitho slept in a room on the first floor, I was the sole occupant of the floor immediately above it.

One night I had been sitting up writing, rather later than usual, and, being very tired, had dropped off to sleep, almost immediately after getting into bed. I woke about two o'clock hearing a curious kind of tapping noise coming along the passage that ran parallel with my bed. Wondering what it could be, I sat up and listened. There were only bare boards outside, and the noise was very clear and resonant, but difficult to analyse. It might have been produced by the very high heels of a lady's boot or shoe, or the bony foot of a skeleton. I could compare it with nothing else. On it came, tap, tap, tap, till it finally seemed to halt outside my door. There was then a pause, during which I could feel somebody or something was listening most earnestly, making sure, I thought, whether I was awake or not, and then a terrific crash on one of the top panels of the door. After this there was silence. I got up, and, somewhat timidly opening the door, for I more than half expected to find myself confronted with something peculiarly dreadful and uncanny, peeped cautiously out. There was nothing to be seen, however; nothing but the cold splendour of the moon, which, shining through a window nearly opposite me, filled the entire passage with its beams. I went into each of the rooms on the landing in turn, but they were all empty, and there was nothing anywhere that could in any way account for what I had heard. In the morning I questioned Mrs Bolitho, but she had heard nothing.

"For a wonder," she said, "I slept very soundly all through the night, and only awoke when it was time to get up."

Two days later I received tidings of the death of my uncle, Colonel John Vize O'Donnell of Trough.[17] He had died almost suddenly, his death occurring a few hours after I had heard the footsteps and the knock.

Three years after this experience I had moved into another house in the same town—also a new house, and also the last in a terrace. At the rear, and on one side of it, was a garden, flanked by a hedge, beyond which were fields that led in almost unbroken succession to the coast. It could not be altogether described as occupying a lonely position, although the fields were little frequented after dusk.

Well, one night my wife and I were awakened about midnight by a series of the most agonising and heart-rending screams, which, if like anything earthly at all, seemed to us to be more like the screams of a woman in the very direst distress. The cries were so terrible and sounded so near to us, almost, in fact, in the room, that we were both horribly alarmed, and hardly knew what to say or think.

"Whatever is happening?" my wife whispered, catching hold of me by the arm, "and what is it?"

"I don't know," was my reply, "unless it is the Banshee, for there is nobody else that could make such a noise."

The screams continued for some seconds, and then died away in one long-drawn-out wail or sob. I waited for some minutes to see if there was a repetition of the sounds, and, there being none, I at length got up, and not, I confess, without considerable apprehensions, went out on to the landing, where I found several of the other inmates of the house collected together discussing with scared faces the screams which they, too, had heard. An examination of the house and grounds was at once made, but nothing was discerned that could in any way account for the sounds, and I adhered to my opinion that it must have been the Banshee; which opinion was very considerably strengthened, when, a few days later, I received the news that an aunt of mine, an O'Donnell, in County Kerry, had passed away

[17] Also spelt Truagh.

within twenty-four hours of the time the screaming had occurred. It is, perhaps, a dozen years or so since we left Cornwall, and my latest experience of the Banshee took place in the house in which we are now living near the Crystal Palace.

The experience occurred in connection with the death of my youngest sister. On the night preceding her decease I dreamed most vividly that I saw the figure of a female dressed in some loose-flowing, fantastic garment come up the path leading to the house, and knock very loudly several times, in quick succession, at the back door. I was going to answer, when a sudden terror held me back.

"It's the Banshee," a voice whispered in my ear, "the Banshee. Don't let her in, she's coming for one of you."

This so startled me that I awoke. I then found that my wife was awake also, trembling all over, and in a great state of excitement.

"Did you hear that tremendous knock?" she whispered.

"What!" I replied. "You don't mean to say there really was a knock? Why, I fancied it was only in my dream."

"You may have dreamt it," she said, "but I didn't—I heard it; it was at this door, not at the front door. I say knock, but it was really a crash—a terrific crash on the top panel of the door."

We anxiously waited to see if there would be a repetition, but, nothing happening, we lay down again, and eventually went to sleep.

On the following day we received a telegram informing us that at ten o'clock that morning my sister had passed away.

Since then, I am glad to relate I have not again come in contact with the Banshee. At the same time, however, there are occasions when I feel very acutely that she is not far away, and I am seldom, if ever, perhaps, absolutely free from an impression that she hovers near at hand, ready to manifest herself the moment either death or disaster threaten any member of my family. Moreover, that she takes a peculiar interest in my personal affairs, I have, alas, only too little reason to doubt.

ADDENDA

In reply to a letter of mine asking for particulars of the Banshee alleged to be attached to the Inchiquin family, I received the following:

"I think the name (of the Banshee) was OBENHEIM, but I am not sure. Two or three people have told me that she appeared before my grandfather's death, but none of them either saw or heard her, but they had met people who did say they had heard her."

Writing also for particulars of the Banshee to a cousin of the head of one of the oldest Irish clans, I received a long letter, from which I will quote the following:

"I have heard 'the Banshee' cry. It is simply like a woman wailing in the most unearthly fashion. At the time an O'Neill was in this house, and she subsequently heard that her eldest brother had died on that night between twelve a.m. and three a.m., when we all of us heard the Banshee wailing. I heard her also at my mother's death, and at the death of my husband's eldest sister. The cry is not always quite the same. When my dear mother died, it was a very low wail which seemed to go round and round the house.

"At the death of one of the great O'Neill family, we located the cry at one end of the house. When my sister-in-law died I was wakened up by a loud scream in my room in the middle of the night. She had died at that instant. I heard the Banshee one day, driving in the country, at a distance. Sometimes the Banshee, who follows old families, is heard by the whole village. Some people say she is red-haired and wears a long flowing white dress. She is supposed to wring her long thick hair. Others say she appears as a small woman dressed in black.

"Such an apparition did appear to me in the daytime before my mother-in-law died."

The writer of this letter has asked me not to publish her name, but I have it by me in case corroboration is needed.

In reference to the O'Donnell Banshee, Chapter XIII., my sister, Petronella O'Donnell, writes:

"I remember vividly my first experience of our Banshee. I had never heard of it at the time, and in fact I have only heard of it in recent years.

"It happened one day that I went into the hall, in the daytime, I forget the exact hour, and as I climbed the stairway, being yet a small child, I happened to look up. There, looking over the rails at the top of the stairway, was an object so horrible that I shudder when I think of it even now. In a greenish halo of light the most terrible head imagination could paint—only this was no imagination, I knew it was a real object—was looking at me with apparently fiendish fire in its light and leering eyes. The head was neither man nor woman's; it was ages old; it might have been buried and dug up again, it was so skull-like and shrunken; its pallor was horrible, grey and mildewy; its hair was long. Its mouth leered, and its light and cruel eyes seemed determined to hurt me to the utmost, with the terror it inspired. I remember how my childish heart rebelled against its cowardice in trying to hurt and frighten so small a child. Gazing back at it in petrified horror, I slowly returned to the room I had come from. I resolved never to tell anyone about it, I was so proud and reserved by nature.

"I had then two secret terrors hidden in my Irish heart. The first one I have never till recently spoken of to anyone; it happened before I saw this awful head. I was asleep, but yet I knew I was *not* asleep. Suddenly, down the road that led to our home in Ireland came an object so terrible that for years after my child's heart used to stand still at the memory of it. The object I saw coming down to our house was a procession—there were several pairs of horses being led by grooms in livery, pulling an old coach with them. It was a large and awful looking old coach! The horses were headless, and the men who led them were headless, and even now as I write, the awful terror of it all comes over me, it was a terror beyond words. I *knew*, I felt certain they had come to cut off my head! This procession of headless things stopped at our door, the men entered the house, chased me up to the very top of it, and then cut off my head! I can remember saying to myself, 'Now I am dead, I am dead, I can suffer no more.'

"They then went back to the coach, and the procession moved away and was lost to view.

"Night after night I lay shivering with terror, for months, for years, there was such a *lurid* horror about this headless procession.

"Some weeks after I saw the head, we heard that our father had been killed about that time in Egypt, murdered it was supposed. My mother died some years afterwards.

"One evening, when I was grown up, we were sitting round the fire with friends, and someone said:

"'I don't believe in ghosts. Have you ever met anyone who

has seen one? I have not!'

"A sudden impulse came over me—never to that moment had I ever mentioned the head—and, leaning forward, I said:

"'I have seen a ghost; I saw the most terrible head when I was a child, looking over the staircase.'

"To my astonishment my sister, who was sitting near me, said:

"'I saw a most terrible head, too, looking over the staircase.'

"I said:

"'When did you see it? I saw it when our father died.'

"And she said:

"'And, *I* saw it when our mother died.'

"In describing it, we found all the details agreed, and learned not long after that it was without doubt our own Banshee we had seen.

"People have said to me that Banshees are heard, not seen. This is not correct, it all depends if one is clairvoyant or clairaudient.

"I remember when my mother was alive, how I came in from a walk one evening and found the whole house in a ferment, the most terrible screaming and crying had been heard pass over the house. Our mother said it must be the Banshee. Sure enough we heard of the death of a very near relation directly after. If I had been present, no doubt I should not only have heard the screams but I should have seen something as well.

"A few years ago in Ireland I was talking about these things, and a relation I had not met before was present. He said to me:

"'But as well as the Banshee do you know that we have a *headless coach* attached to our family; it is proceeded by men, who lead the horses, and none of them have heads.'

"Like a flash came that never-to-be-forgotten vision of that awful procession I had seen as a child, and of which I had never made any mention till then. I remember now that after I saw the headless coach we heard that our grandmother was dead. I believe that the headless coach belongs to her family.

"PETRONELLA O'DONNELL."

The headless coach referred to in the foregoing account comes to us, I believe, from the Vize family. My grandmother before her marriage was Sarah Vize, daughter of John Vize of Donegal, Glenagad and Limerick. Her sister Frances married her cousin, David Roche of Carass (see Burke's "Landed Gentry of Ireland," under Maunsell family, and Burke's "Peerage under Roche"), their son being Sir David Roche, Bart.

The great-great-grandmother of Sarah Vize was Mary, daughter of Butler of the house of the Earl Glengall Cahir. Sarah Vize's mother, my great-grandmother, before her marriage was Sarah Maunsell, granddaughter of William Maunsell of Ballinamona, County Cork, the fifth son of Colonel Thomas Maunsell of Mocollop.

In the accompanying genealogical tree, tracing the descent of the O'Donnells of Trough from Niall of the Nine Hostages, the O'Briens of Thomond and the O'Rourkes of Brefui, may be found the basis upon which my family's claim to the dual Banshee rests.

The original may be seen in the office of the King of Arms, Dublin. The following is merely an extract:

Niall of the Nine Hostages.
King of Ireland
|
Conall Gulban
|
Feargus
|
Leadna, Prince of Tirconnell
|
Feargus
|
Lughaidb, and from

him, in direct descent, to Foirdhealbhach an Fhiona O'Donnhnaill, who had two sons, the elder, Shane Luirg and the younger, Niall Garbh. From Niall Garbh the illustrious Red Hugh and his brother Rory, Earl of Tirconnell, were descended, from Shane Luirg, whose rank as "The O'Donnell" was taken by his younger brother, presumably the stronger man of the two, the Trough O'Donnells are descended.

The line goes on thus:

Shane Luirg
|
Art O'Domnhnail (ob. circa 1490)
|
Niall O'Domnhnaill (ob. circa 1525)
|
Foirdhealbhach O'Domnhnaill *m.* Julia Maguire (ob. 1552)
|
Shane *m.* Rosa, d. of Hugh O'Donnell (ob. 1581)
|
Hugh O'Donnell of Limerick *m.* Maria, d. of Donat O'Brien of the House of Thomond (ob. 1610)
|
Edmund, of Limerick (ob. 1651) *m.* Bridget, d. of O'Rourk of the House of Brefui
|
James, of Limerick (ob. 1680) *m.* Helena, d. of James Sarsfield, great-uncle of Patrick Sarsfield, Earl of Lucan
|
John *m.* Margaret, d. of Thomas Creagh of Limerick
|
James *m.* Christiana, d. of William Stritch of Limerick
|
John (ob. 1780) *m.* Deborah, d. of William Anderson of Tipperary
|
Henry Anderson O'Don- *m.* Domina Jan, daughter of nephew
nell (ob. 1840)   of Shah of Persia
|
Gen. Sir C. R. O'Donnell , *m.* Catherine Anne, d. of Gen. P.
K.C.B., and Member of the   Murray, nephew of the Earl of
Irish Academy (ob. 1870)   Elibank

[*]John, of Limerick and Bal- *m.* Sarah Elliot
timore, U.S.A (ob. 1805) | of Baltimore, U.S.A

Elliot, of Limerick (ob. 1836) *m.* Sarah Vize,
       of Limerick
|
Rev. Henry O'Donnell
|
Elliot (youngest son)

For particulars of the pedigree see Vol. X., p. 327, Genealogias, in the Office of Ulster King of Arms, Dublin.

From Niall to Shane Luirg, see Register XV., p. 5; from Shane to my grandfather, Elliot, see Register XXIII., p. 286; and down to myself, see "Sheridan," p. 323.

Referring to the Banshee prior to my aunt's death (see Chapter XIII.) my wife writes:

> "I certainly remember, one night, when we were living in Cornwall, hearing a most awful scream, a scream that rose and fell, and ended in a long-drawn-out wail of agony. I have never heard any other sound at all like it, and therefore cannot think that it could have been anything earthly. At the time, however, I did think that possibly the scream was that of a woman being murdered, and did not rest until my husband, with other inmates of our house, had made a thorough search of the garden and premises.

> "Shortly after we had had this experience, we heard of the death, in Ireland, of one of my husband's aunts.

> "I also recollect that one night, shortly before we received the news of my sister-in-law's death, I heard a crash on our bedroom door. It was so loud that it quite shook the room, and my husband, apparently wakened by it, told me he had dreamed that the Banshee had come and was knocking for admittance. This happened not very long ago, when we were living in Norwood.

> "ADA O'DONNELL."

ENDNOTES

[*] John O'Donnell of Baltimore's eldest son, Columbus, had a daughter, Eleanora, who married Adrian Iselin of New York, and their grand-daughter, Norah, is the present Princess Coleredo Mansfeldt.

Lector House believes that a society develops through a two-fold approach of continuous learning and adaptation, which is derived from the study of classic literary works spread across the historic timeline of literature records. Therefore, we aim at reviving, repairing and redeveloping all those inaccessible or damaged but historically as well as culturally important literature across subjects so that the future generations may have an opportunity to study and learn from past works to embark upon a journey of creating a better future.

This book is a result of an effort made by Lector House towards making a contribution to the preservation and repair of original ancient works which might hold historical significance to the approach of continuous learning across subjects.

HAPPY READING & LEARNING!

LECTOR HOUSE LLP
E-MAIL: lectorpublishing@gmail.com

9 789390 198665